MW01626428

An *Unexpected* Ride

The Art of Celebrating Life While Living with a Disability

Foreword By George Hage

By Non Reyes

Husband, Father, Artist, Writer, Disability Advocate

An Unexpected Ride
The Art of Celebrating Life While Living with a Disability

Print ISBN: 978-1-61206-342-3
eBook ISBN: 978-1-61206-343-0
Audiobook ISBN: 978-1-61206-344-7

Printed in the United States of America

To my beloved wife, Sylvia, whose unwavering love and strength have been my foundation.

To my children, Jacob and Isabella, who remind me daily of life's beauty and resilience.

To my precious grandchildren, who fill my days with wonder and my heart with hope. May you always know the strength of love and the power of perseverance.

You are my greatest blessings, and this book is for you.

Contents

Foreword

As a retired occupational therapist with 43 years of experience in rehab, I can unequivocally say that no one has influenced my career and my humanity more positively than my friend and brother, Non Reyes.

I first met Non less than two weeks after his accident while he was waiting to transfer to Rancho Los Amigos Rehabilitation Center in Downey, California. At the time, I worked at Elk's Rehabilitation Hospital in Boise, Idaho. A co-worker asked me to meet a newly injured C3-4 quadriplegic at the local hospital intensive care unit. He was at St. Luke's Hospital, located just across the street from where I worked.

Walking into his hospital room, I saw he was using a ventilator to breathe and was unable to speak due to a recent tracheotomy. I smiled and introduced myself. Non smiled back and nodded. It was understandably a short visit, but a very significant one for me. I have a vague recollection—due to a photograph—of Non, his wife, Sylvia, and 2-year-old son, Jacob, sitting on the nightstand. As I left, I remember feeling both heartache and compassion for him, his family, and the long, hard road ahead. Little did I know he would become one of my closest friends over a span of 30-plus years. Nor did I imagine he would inspire countless people, locally in Idaho's Treasure Valley and also in some of the poorest countries of the world. It was not only his newly found artistic talent that was so impressive, but also his faith, courage, and desire to live the life he was dealt with warmth and the passion to make others feel comfortable with his disability.

Non has proved himself to be just as much a talented writer as he is a mouth artist. You will find that he writes, paints, and lives with wisdom, compassion, adventure, and heart. As an occupational therapist, I've been around situations similar to Non's for more than four decades. I would recommend this book to anyone working or planning to work in physical rehabilitation, whether you're a therapist, nurse, social worker, physician, or student. I would also recommend it to those in any community connected with individuals with disabilities and their families. You will learn valuable insights and realities about the many challenges facing your patients. I recommend this book to anyone suffering a significant loss, knowing life will never be the same. You will find the strength to move forward and dream new dreams. I recommend this book to anyone needing a little encouragement or inspiration. Non's life exemplifies courage and inspiration.

I watched Non write this book over the last few years, with setbacks in health, lack of consistent available caregivers, limited time out of bed, and all the challenges of life. One of the things I've found impressive was his patience and determination not to give up. What makes it more impressive is the tedious process he used to put words on paper.

You will feel a variety of emotions as you read this book. As I shared his story on 11 different trips to the developing world, the initial response I heard, more than any other was, "Wow." Just "Wow." That may be your response too. Prepare to be inspired.

—George Hage, retired Occupational Therapist

How I Wrote This Book

This book was written using a hands-free mouse alternative that allows users to control their computer cursor by simply moving their head. With a reflective dot placed on my forehead and a pneumatic switch connected via a tube in my mouth to this device, I can point the cursor on my computer screen and trigger a left mouse-click with a sip of the tube, and a right mouse-click with a puff. I also used an on-screen keyboard to type one sip (one letter) at a time.

This process has been tedious and often disheartening at times. I accidentally lost complete sections of my book by highlighting a section and then breathing in, and POOF, it was gone. But every letter typed meant not giving in or giving up. This device gave me independence and freedom and has helped me connect with friends and family like everyone else.

Introduction

Daddy, Scratch My Back

August 1993

As I lay in bed alone, staring out the window and dreaming of days long past, I faintly hear the sound of my son playing in the next room. Months earlier, he had been always animated and excited when I got home from work. He'd eagerly climb on my shoulders before I could get my coat off, tell me about his day, and we would play hide-and-seek, one of our favorite games. It always made me smile when he concealed only part of his body during our games. Because he couldn't see me, he thought he was invisible. When it was my turn to hide, I would jump out and scare him, and his smiles and laughter never disappointed.

My son giggled often and always had fun. He was also a talker, full of questions, ideas, and wishes as we played the typical roles of father and son. Being an only child, he didn't have to fight for our attention or wait long for answers to his questions. I loved being a father, enjoying those interactions as I taught and learned from him. His requests for hugs and to ride on my shoulders reminded me that he felt safe in my arms.

As a young adult filled with self-doubt, I didn't trust much. But I tried to adapt to life, to keep moving forward, to hope. Then, I became a husband and a father, wanting to be better with my loved ones than I was alone. I loved the idea of protecting them from harm; it was comforting. As a parent, you hold someone's life in your hands with your influence, a lifelong responsibility. Still, being a husband and dad made me happy.

However, I am not myself anymore. Now, each time my son bounces into my room regret fills my broken heart. I am constantly worried because our lives have changed so much. I feel I don't have all the answers for him like before and am certain I can't give him what he needs.

I spend most of every hopeless day in bed, reliving memories I hope will mend my broken heart. Laying here this morning was no different. Jacob often pops into the room to ask a question or share a toy. His smiles and voice are a solace. But when he interrupted his play and bounced into my crowded room today, there was an unusual angst in his presence. He spoke and made a simple request.

"Daddy, scratch my back," Jacob said.

My heart sank.

Instantly, I felt heavy, suffocating air envelop me. It was my nightmare compressed into a few seconds in this tiny room. And I couldn't wake up. I was at a loss for words, unsure how to address what was obvious. I CANNOT scratch his back. I will NEVER be able to scratch his back!

As I searched for a response that protected his innocence and shielded him from the pain and heartache I felt, the reality of my situation tore at my soul. Life had taken a tragic turn for us. I could not move, much less scratch his back, because I broke my neck in a terrible accident—altering my understanding of fairness. I wanted to yell at God, at myself—at everything. Giving Jacob an honest answer to his request was more than I could handle. And it would only lead to questions I was not ready for. More than that, I didn't want him to understand my internal anguish. The emotions were dark and filled with self-loathing. I didn't want to disappoint my son more than I already had.

My new reality is that I am paralyzed. I have no movement below my shoulders. I cannot raise an arm, bend a finger, or move a toe. If you squeeze my hand, I can't feel it. I have many chronic medical problems that can be life-threatening. And I cannot take care of myself.

My days are long, structured, and occupied with caregivers and healthcare workers—making everyday life overwhelming and my outlook bleak and uncertain. At 26, I live in a senior housing facility with my wife, Sylvia, and son, Jacob. As I bargain with God for a miracle to be whole again, memories of being a good dad are all that remain.

Whenever I find myself alone, I reminisce about the carefree days of my former life. I enjoyed playing sports in high school, participating in city league softball, football, and basketball, and sneaking away to play a round of golf. Growing up among active cousins, I played flag football on Thanksgiving Day. It was part of a tradition I always looked forward to—laughter, love, and connection—the best parts of life.

I also look back on fighting fires for the BLM, the craziness of my college days (some of the best and worst of my life) at ISU and BSU, and the rewards of being a high school tutor. The memories of a former active life provide a brief but unfair escape from my reality. I wish I could heal and be alive, invincible, and able to overcome again. In my heart, I know healing isn't possible. Praying only makes me feel forsaken because, after every counterfeit dream, I wake up in my hospital bed, unable to move, battling my thoughts. At times, I wonder if I should have died.

Able-bodied memories bring pain and remorse because I can no longer hold Jacob or provide for him or Sylvia. I can no longer affect change to fix anything. Things weren't perfect before. But at least there was a future I could work toward. Now, memories remind me of how good my life was and all the dreams I lost. Memories leave me with sadness and guilt for the choices I made, and a nagging emptiness I feel will never go away.

So, when Jacob bounced into the room and stood alongside my bed, the torrent of emotions overwhelmed me. I fought back tears. My role as a father no longer applied. I didn't have a response for him when he asked me to scratch his back. Sensing my hesitation, loss of words, and obvious distress, Jacob, with a look of consternation, rescued me.

He said, "With your whiskers, Daddy!"

Then he climbed onto my hospital bed. And with a partial back bridge, he leaned into my face and I scratched his back with my chin—tears slowly trickling down my face. It was so simple yet so profound.

Jacob saw what I could do, not what I couldn't.

The roles of teacher and student reversed for a second when he spoke today. I was tired of feeling sad and hopeless. And his words helped me accept that I could still be his father.

Although my physical abilities have changed, and I can't carry my son on my shoulders anymore, he still sees me as Daddy. Even though we live in a senior care facility filled with medical equipment and supplies, Jacob views this tiny apartment as his home. Despite my rigid daily routine with caregivers completing their shifts and healthcare workers delivering their services, he adjusted, learned their names, and was eager to help.

I know I have a huge challenge ahead. There will be depressing realities and frequent disappointments, and I will battle numerous demons, often falling hard. Yet, amidst this struggle, I have begun to hope for the strength to pick myself up again. Life feels different; my heart is not as heavy.

Though I can't golf with my son, I can teach him how to play. I might not show him how to swing a baseball bat, but I can be his coach and biggest fan. I may not be able to hug him, but he can hug me. My hope stirred when Jacob showed me that I could still scratch his back. I have much to give, and I hope to be the man I always aspired to be—just a slightly different version.

After November 9, 1992, trauma struck my body, my family, my life, and my hope as I lay critically wounded. Yet, nine months later, my son has helped me envision a possible future. As a young, 26-year-old man, my rigid view of life—of all I could conquer and achieve—was shattered. But today, when I scratched Jacob's back, it felt like a prayer was answered.

Chapter 1

Growing Up

I grew up in a small, quintessential Northwest town of less than 1,500 people. We moved there from the Midwest in 1973 after my uncle convinced my father he needed to be near family. Helping paint a quaint picture, the town had a drugstore, a post office, and a mom-and-pop hamburger joint called the Polar Bear that had a Skylab pinball machine and a jukebox that—for some reason—always seemed to be playing "Brick House" by the Commodores. You could also use the drive-up window or the side window for walk-up orders to buy a banana split or an ice cream cone. There were two gas stations in town where you could air up your bike tires and fix a flat, and a hardware store where you would run into a farmer drinking a cup of coffee as he waited for the materials he needed to fix something on the farm. Two markets I worked in as an early teen completed the picture of small-town America. I have fond memories of growing up there. Life was simple.

There was no judgement or stigma about being part of such a small community. Nor did our family feel the stereotypes of living in a modest 12-by-60-foot trailer. In it, the AC unit—permanently mounted in the living room window—created a hum suitable for a movie sound stage. However, it made the hot summer nights more bearable. Space was limited. The dining table in our linoleum-clad kitchen was shoved against the wall—allowing just enough room to walk around it. It would have seated all five family members if placed in the middle of the eight-by-eight-foot room. But the arrangement provided access to the narrow hall leading to two of three small bedrooms and a bathroom. Alongside the trailer, we had a tiny side yard that we made the most of when we were young.

Everyone in town knew our names and watched out for us—unafraid to scold us if we did something wrong. The adage "It takes a village to raise a child," applied to our experience. And we were better for the type of environment we grew up in. With few worries, we rode our bikes all over town and in the countryside, ran through sprinklers, played hide-and-seek, and kick-the-can. We also played baseball until it was too dark to see the ball—learning the hard way when it was time to quit because we often got into trouble if we stayed out too late. There were few distractions.

Sundays played a big part of the security we felt. Our entire extended family would attend my uncle Ramiro's church—one of several in the community. Being there felt like a weekly family reunion with a few other members and friends mixed in teaching us Sunday school and how to behave. After Sunday school, we listened to my uncle Ramiro deliver his weekly sermon. It was usually direct, sometimes harsh—because it included a personal lesson or two—but something we would take home to remind us of our belief and faith. At church, we understood the blessings of family. We knew there was always someone to watch over us—someone we could turn to. I was particularly close to my cousins, uncles, and aunts. The older cousins filled atypical familial roles, influencing and protecting us in various ways. I was thankful for their love and the warm embrace that was always there. Growing up in the church provided a foundation that would affect my entire life.

At home, I was the oldest of three. And for as long as I remember, I felt the need to protect my sister, Mirna, and brother, Ray. It was my responsibility as a big brother to look out for them. I remember walking them to school and making tiny cereal boxes for us on Saturdays—the kind you just add milk to after cutting the box down the middle. I also recall helping with the occasional homework assignment, playing with them, and teasing them too. As I did my best to fulfill my role, most of our pains and worries were ordinary, not usually having to protect them from any specific outside threat.

Instead, we were affected by dysfunction. Our parents were typical in most ways. Our mother was funny, determined, and always saw the best in things. Our father was a personable man who taught us to shake hands and show respect with a "yes, sir" and "yes, ma'am." He enjoyed a good laugh and, later in life, reminded me that I met my angel when I began dating my wife. He had so many likable qualities, and I loved him for all he taught us. They were loving parents.

On the other side of the coin, however, our father wrestled with something that drove him to excessive drinking, causing angst, fear, and worry in the family.

We all coped in our own ways—each of our experiences and perspective different. Young and unable to do much more than pretend and internalize each detrimental experience, I focused on trying to keep my brother and sister from feeling the way I did.

Although much of the time at home was positive and normal, alcoholism was a regular reminder that brought police visits, exhausted mornings, and slurred speech encounters with Dad—issues that evoked many confusing and unwanted emotions. They happened frequently enough that my mom facetiously used a word to describe my father when he drank too much and became someone we sometimes feared. She would say he was being "ugly," accompanied by a smirk. To her credit, it was her way of making light of something that was difficult for all of us—to show a brave face and keep from crumbling under the weight she constantly bore.

In response to his Mr. Hyde persona on weekends—and sometimes during the week—we would pretend to be asleep when he arrived home later than 7 p.m., worried about the different person he became. There were also times when fear and angst raced down a narrow road at 80 miles an hour, us in tow, longing for normal.

I don't know if his drinking became worse or if I just became increasingly sensitive to how it affected me and my family. But as I got older, there were more confrontations between him and me. To protect my brother, sister, and mom as much as possible, I attempted to step into the middle of anxious moments, even those that didn't initially involve me. In my mind, I handled the confrontation well when I diverted his focus from them to me without anyone getting pushed around. Sometimes it worked better than others. But it never felt good no matter how it ended. The hurt was always there on the inside—building distrust and a chip on my shoulder.

At odds, and as confrontations increased, he became less scary as my perception of him changed. This was mostly because I needed to see something else in him to be okay with the whole situation. But also because I felt stronger having confronted him. The need to focus on his gifts with less fear clouding my vision allowed me to set aside my antipathy. As my confidence in my ability to change and redirect sadness away from my family grew, so did my resolve.

There was also goodness. Childhood memories of him dancing with my mom on Sunday mornings conversely added to the warmth and affection he brought to our family. Amidst the despair, his gifts and these happy memories helped paint history in a different light—as he was more than just an alcoholic.

But you could still count on bad days—seemingly more impactful than the good ones. They seemed bolder and more memorable because these moments tore down rather than uplifted us.

My father garnered respect in the community for his personality, social skills, sense of humor, and intelligence. He was also an athlete and loved sports. So I focused on our similarities to make sense of our strained relationship. After I left home we seemed to be less at odds as we talked about football, basketball, and every other sport throughout the year.

We were each affected by the raw environment in our own specific ways. Yet, despite the challenges, my sister, brother, and I managed to maintain relatively typical relationships growing up. Being four years younger than me, my sister and I naturally fell into that big brother/little sister dynamic. We share a similar stubbornness, a quick sense of humor, and a mutual appreciation for learning new things. On the surface, our relationship looked like that of any typical siblings.

My brother, just a year younger than me, experienced everything at home right alongside me—both the highs and the lows—through a similar lens. Ever the joker, he used humor as a shield, his sharp wit a weapon against our worries. Although turmoil stained nearly everything around us, it didn't seem to leave any visible marks on our relationships with each other.

On a lighter note, my siblings also enjoy following sports, but although they might argue otherwise, I was the one who truly lived and breathed it. For me, sports were more than just a hobby—they were therapy. It wasn't just about winning or losing; it was an escape, a way to channel all the emotions I couldn't otherwise express. Even in the heat of midsummer, when the temperature soared to 100 degrees, I begged my brother to play catch. To his credit, he usually went along with it, even though I'm sure he had better things to do. Those moments, under the blazing sun, tossing the ball back and forth, were simple but meant everything to me. They were a way to connect, to feel grounded when life was anything but.

The environment we grew up in undoubtedly shaped us, though the degree of influence varied. Ray and I, being older, felt the weight of it more intensely. We were more aware of the undercurrents, more attuned to the tension that ran beneath the surface. That difference in age also meant I didn't spend as much time with my sister. We were close, but she was still figuring things out while I was already caught up in the swirl of everything around us.

On the other hand, my brother and I were inseparable, especially during the long summer months. We spent those days together, sharing the highs and lows, from the mundane to the mischievous. Whether we were sneaking out, pulling harmless pranks, or just getting into trouble in that way kids do, we were always a team. Sometimes we crossed the line, and sometimes we got caught—but we were in it together. Those moments of shared rebellion strengthened our bond, building a foundation that remained solid even when everything else felt shaky.

One hot summer afternoon in the late '70s, my parents were out for ice cream and a drive in the country. They did this sometimes to beat the heat of a late summer afternoon. More often, the outings repaired trust injured the night before. The warmth of the summer contrasted with the cold of the conflicts, the quiet hum of the engine with the harsh words, and the simple pleasure of the countryside had a way of smoothing over the tensions that inevitably built up at home.

While slowly driving among the planted fields and irrigation ditches, catching the summer breeze, they noticed a few kids on the road ahead. From a distance, they could see they were young and diving headfirst into a deep, fast-moving irrigation canal. My mom couldn't believe what she was seeing: young children, unsupervised, playing in this dangerous place. "Where are their parents?" she asked out loud. Her instincts kicked in, imagining the worst potential outcomes—angered because their families undoubtedly didn't know where they were. *How could they be out here?* she thought.

As they approached the bridge, my parents exchanged a glance, both of them worked up and ready to give these reckless kids a stern talking-to. My mom had her speech all but rehearsed in her head—how irresponsible it was, how their parents would be furious if they knew, how they were putting themselves in danger for no good reason. But as the car drew closer, she recognized two of the kids standing on the edge of the bridge, nervously glancing back toward the approaching car. She exclaimed, "It's Ray and Hernan!" They weren't just random neighborhood delinquents—they were *her* kids.

When my parents were within yelling distance, we—and our friends—got an earful. We were embarrassed and all told to go home. Our friends only pretended to heed the warning—getting out of the water only to jump right back in after we left. When Ray and I returned home, we were scolded again and punished. However, this didn't stop us from taking risks and acting foolishly like typical kids. Mom would often remind us of that day to keep us in line.

My sister, on the other hand, rarely got in trouble with us. She knew how to get in trouble all by herself! Kidding aside, I hope her safer, more naive experience made her less aware of the issues at home, and that her stresses weren't like mine. I hope the influence I had on her was positive and that she saw in me a good student, a disciplined athlete, and a big brother who could make her mad at times but was always ready to stand up for her.

As much as I hope that I was there for them, I am so grateful for them being there for me. Both my siblings have been strong supports when I needed them.

A core influence, my mother was the rock for my siblings and me growing up. Her stature—just four feet eleven inches tall—belied her resilience. And like most kids, we took her unwavering support for granted. Throughout her life there were lean times, but my mom always took on a second or third job to make ends meet. She also made sure we could learn music, play sports, and attend church camp. There was a consistency—a constant source of normal associated with my mom that my siblings and I felt.

When we tore our jeans, she patched them right back up. And when she brought hot dogs to change up dinner, or when we needed a reassuring kindness to remind us it would be okay, she was there, seemingly unphased, every single day. As she faced stresses and hardships with strength and perseverance, she planted seeds of hope for the future without knowing the impact she had on us. Whether at work or taking care of us, even what was difficult seemed tolerable—indeed enjoyable to her. Her outlook on life has always been to find the proverbial silver lining in any situation—to whistle while you work.

Once I turned 13, I began working summers in the fields thinning beets, topping onions, and digging out corrugates to help buy school clothes. It was a responsibility that helped bring income and helped my mom. I felt good about making my own money—grown up. My mom joined me. She would work out in the fields after finishing her regular job with the school district—always doing extra as she cared for us. Her company out in the heat and extreme conditions made me feel better about everything.

From a young teen's perspective, the environment while working in the fields was dirty, hot, and just plain uncomfortable. But others worked in the fields. I wasn't special. For my mom, however, the job seemed to have little effect on her, unlike us kids who would rather be swimming or sleeping in for the summer. For her, whistling while you work wasn't just a metaphor for being happy in the tough spots. Mom always whistled while she worked, literally.

Summer temperatures in Idaho can reach over one hundred degrees—especially in August. Detasseling corn, one of the more miserable jobs, was on our late summer schedule. For this job, arms and necks had to be fully covered to protect from the blazing sun and itchy pollen—a perfect combination of heat and discomfort that swayed many from doing the job. Conditions were miserable for the mostly teenage crew we worked with. Everyone expressed their distress. Mom, on the other hand, would walk out of a row of corn, dripping with sweat, singing and whistling. It seemed that very little broke my mom. My friends asked why she was like that, unfazed by the tough conditions. The only thing I could say was, "She's just happy."

Looking back, I understand that she was more than that. She was sincerely grateful for all the good despite the bad. She didn't take things for granted. And we learned from her attitude to stay positive through hardship.

The story book environment described everything we did: riding our bikes everywhere, playing in the schoolyard sprinklers, getting into trouble, and playing Little League baseball all summer long. Playing baseball against teams from neighboring towns helped us forge bonds with both teammates and opponents alike. And sometimes, we'd venture miles away on our bikes to meet new friends, grab an ice cream cone, and munch on French fries.

We also explored the local gravel pit—an empty lot that had mounds we could ride over—traversed back roads, and weaved through potato, beet, and hop fields, embarking on countless unknown adventures. These experiences were the best joys of childhood.

Growing up held a montage of happy memories: baseball, music, school, friends, family, and church.

Yet amidst the wholesome and positive experiences, there was the ever-present drama at home. It was challenging for me to reconcile that the good could be diluted by the bad, shaping my life.

Beyond the embrace of family, friends, and small-town nostalgia, school provided a significant refuge for my siblings and me. Teachers, classmates, and the activities we engaged in nurtured and influenced us, offering warmth akin to a loving hug. In a small school with fewer teachers and students, the environment felt more welcoming. Participation in sports and school clubs was accessible because each person mattered to make things function smoothly.

School became a sanctuary where I could escape the chaos and uncertainty that plagued our home life—where I could pretend everything was okay. Unlike at home, pressures seemed to dissipate within the school's supportive environment. It was a place where I felt safe.

Participation in high school sports became a significant source of confidence and a welcome escape from accumulated angst. On the playing field, there were no distractions—just the game, with its rules and known challenges. As I honed discipline, teamwork, and sportsmanship, my love for sports, particularly baseball, blossomed. Vivid memories of diving for a ball up the middle, throwing out the runner at first, or turning a single into a double transport me back to cherished moments.

Football and basketball also provided a hopeful escape from the challenges brewing in my mind, allowing me to tune out everything else for hours at a time. I may not have been the most talented or fastest player on any team, but I always found a way to get open, make a play, and contribute.

Teammates, the school environment, and game days were like medicine, offering a healing escape. However, sometimes my struggles followed me onto the field—especially when my father showed up to watch a baseball or football game, arriving "ugly." The fear that his presence would expose our family's dysfunction was paralyzing. I would hold my breath, whether from the field or the dugout, worried about potential incidents.

But my baseball coach, Mr. Cagle, was a guardian angel in those moments. He intercepted any potential issues before they could escalate. I remember vividly how he walked over to my dad's car in the middle of a game, somehow preventing any embarrassing outbursts caused by my father's drinking. Mr. Cagle always seemed to know exactly what to do or say. Typically, the outcome of such encounters was my dad driving away and my coach returning to the team, often with a reassuring smile on his face as he approached me.

Like the rest of the country, Friday nights belonged to high school football in our town, another sport that distracted me. I relished running routes, reading the defense, and slipping into open spaces. The anticipation built throughout game day, fueled by pep rallies and the encouraging treats from the pep squad.

One memorable Friday evening, our team faced off against a local rival known for their talented athletes. We had played a solid first half but found ourselves trailing late in the game with our backs against the wall. As we gained momentum moving down the field, Coach Lynn called a crucial play involving me—a quick five-yard slant route to secure a much-needed first down.

Just before the snap, I noticed the defense adjusting, seemingly creating an opening for an easy catch and the necessary yardage. However, I failed to see a linebacker shifting into position to cover my route. The ball was snapped, and I executed my slant, diving for a slightly off-target pass. Vulnerable and focused on securing the catch, I was blindsided by the linebacker's perfectly timed hit. And the impact knocked the wind out of me, leaving me sprawled on the field, gasping for air.

The referee stopped the game and told me to stay down, waving over to the sidelines for someone to assist me. But I wasn't thinking about the temporary pain as I gasped for the air the tackle had knocked out of me. More troubling was that the play caught my father's attention in the stands. His response was disproportionate—yelling without a filter as I lay trying to take a deep breath. Keenly aware of the commotion, I could only focus on his voice, knowing he wouldn't stop yelling until I got up. Even though he heard my aunt raising her voice: "Look, brother. He's okay," that wasn't enough to quiet him. So, I stood up—shaky—despite the referee's plea to take my time. I staggered to the sidelines with some help, and my father began to calm down. But I knew I had to stay up to keep him off the field. Still unsteady, I started to slump. That's when I felt a strong arm come alongside me, holding me up. Then I heard the words, "It's okay. I have you." Looking up at Coach Cagle, I noticed a tear roll down his cheek. He said, "It's okay, I know," as the moment dissipated into nothing. In the stands, my aunt convinced my father to stay away from the field, and the game continued without more unwanted attention.

Mr. Cagle was my coach. But the kindness he displayed sums up how he protected not just me, but all of us. And the incident further cemented in me a trust, a safe place I felt at school. I am thankful he was in my life, and I will always remember his compassion and how he seemed to understand and know what to do.

Throughout my life, there was always someone who lent an arm or shoulder to help lessen the disquiet. Extended family, friends, and heroes helped us keep our heads up. Guardians and protectors have kept me from falling with an encouraging word of support—especially family.

Our Wednesday youth group gathering was a constant, weekly family event during my teenage years that gave support and encouragement away from school. The company of cousins and friends was something else that helped smooth the abrasions caused at home. The close bunch gathered often and had fun camping, tubing, and roller skating. We also went to places to be inspired by altruistic selfless people. Challenged by a deeper message during our outings, we learned of faith, about ourselves, and how others cope with adversity.

Sometimes, the chip on my shoulder prevented me from fully embracing what I learned. Much of what we experienced and listened to only reinforced my doubts, as I hoped for change without seeing it. I often wondered how the stories and messages we heard applied to us. Yet, despite this, the lessons accumulated.

In 1982, my cousin Maria arranged for our youth group to hear an inspirational speaker during an outing—a story I will never forget. The speaker, Joni Eareckson Tada, spoke of a diving accident that left her paralyzed, with only partial use of her arms. In the crowded arena, Joni shared the story of her life before the accident and the battle to live again afterward. Despite all her struggles, she talked about being thankful, finding hope, and following her faith—a faith that helped her recover from such a tragic event. She also spoke about finding purpose in sharing her faith and discovering art. Her message stayed with me more than I could have ever imagined.

You never fully understand the significance of the events that influence your life as they unfold.

Most of these impactful moments occur without your immediate awareness. During my high school years, certain experiences had a weighted influence on my future. Even though high school only comprises about 6% of a 70-year-long life, a small enough amount of time that common sense suggests shouldn't affect you all that much, my time was full of key moments.

One of the most significant moments in my life took place in the fall of 1981 when a friend asked me to accompany him to a Catholic dance. He mentioned he wanted to meet a certain pretty girl but didn't want to go alone. His invitation, however, came with one condition. I had to promise I wouldn't talk or dance with her. Since I wasn't doing anything that weekend, I agreed to keep myself in check while serving as his wingman.

When we arrived that Saturday evening and walked through the hall leading to the church gymnasium, he reminded me of the deal I made. I smiled and thought to myself, he's very serious about this.

The gymnasium, decorated with a few streamers, had a small, raised dance platform that screamed of the 80s. A table to the right of the entrance held a punch bowl and cookies. Someone was greeting people as they walked in. There weren't many there yet. But I decided to enjoy myself and shake a leg. As more people trickled in, I was chatting with someone when the girl my friend had told me about walked in with a couple of friends.

I hung back, sticking to my promise, and watched as my friend made his way over to her. Despite my agreement, I felt a strong urge to join in. I resisted, but I remember every detail about her. She wore a white blouse with ruffled cuffs under a tan corduroy jacket with elbow patches. Her tight khaki pants were tucked into cute little boots, and her big, wavy hair framed her beautiful face.

The two hours at the dance flew by, leaving me with a memory that would stay with me for years. I didn't realize it then, but she had left an indelible mark on me, eventually finding her way into my heart. In a way, I'm grateful Henry made me promise not to talk or dance with her that night; I probably would have messed it up and missed out on one of the most meaningful parts of my life. For now, though, life went on without her.

Band, drama, and student government added to the milieu of distractions at school. The refuge served as a guide. And I did okay academically and athletically, graduating with honors and earning several scholarships. These achievements enabled me to move on and enroll in university as an engineering major. The transition to college felt positive in many ways, making that short stretch of life feel both typical and extraordinary.

Growing up with angst, worry, and fear, however, leaves a mark. Guilt followed me to college, as I worried about abandoning my family after high school. I felt I had left them behind and wouldn't be there to provide a buffer between them and dread. I left reluctantly, with scholarships, enough confidence to wish for change, and a handful of dreams.

With a decent plan and some hope, I looked forward to a new chapter in my life, trying to dismiss the emotional and psychological baggage I carried. I was still waiting to lose after a win, seeing life as a zero-sum game. The fear of success was a concept I didn't understand, but I also didn't want to fail because of the blame I placed on my unsettled childhood. I was conflicted.

As it turns out, some of the character flaws I faulted my father for while growing up—alcoholism, not following through, running away, not being there—became my own. They needed attention, but I had no idea how to address them at school, alone. His influence was profound in my life.

The paradox is that he taught me valuable lessons, like shaking hands and practicing good manners, the contention I experienced left invisible scars that provided an antithetical foundation for a happy life. There was plenty of both—good and bad. Which parts should I tackle, and which should I dismiss? I didn't know how to begin. It wasn't simple, especially for a fundamentally flawed 18-year-old.

The first year of college, I eagerly dove into the educational experience, playing intramural sports, trying out for track, working a small job, and loving the whole university environment. Dreams of a perfect future without angst and struggle encouraged me as I started school. And I did well, both academically and otherwise. But my past affected my behavior because the transition from high school to university didn't address the brokenness I brought from home. As time passed, I struggled with drinking, used poor judgment at school, and got into another big clash at home while there for the summer.

Impulsivity prevailed, and I quit school after my sophomore year to go to California. The time in California was not a solution to my issues—merely a reaction to something I didn't want to cope with. But the months there were important—a time to reflect. After less than a year, reminded of how much I loved Idaho, I returned—appreciative of fewer cars, more trees, less chaos, and family.

Making my way from home to school, California to Idaho, was a long roundabout journey, hoping for change. Back at home, I wanted to get back in the game—get a job, return to school, and work on myself. So, I began by finding employment. One of my jobs, working for a good friend's dad, was a good start. And getting a job as a high school equivalency tutor also felt like I had made the right choice. While working and starting over, I began to find a sense of purpose and direction.

Chapter 2

Bridges to Adulthood

I would no longer be living back home. The town I loved for my family, friends, coaches, teachers, and church—all that guided and nurtured me throughout my childhood—felt oddly unfamiliar. Not because I didn't care, but because I had to maintain distance from memories that made me feel like I was not good enough. The memories were still fresh.

School wasn't an option either, at least not right away. Since returning to Wilder didn't fit, I chose to move down the road to a neighboring town of 18,000 people, where there was more opportunity for work, education, and fun. Living close to the extended family that supported me growing up was comforting. So, I settled in and reconnected with summer employment, fighting wildfires with the BLM. I also worked in a small factory and later found employment painting with friends.

Moving in with buddies I worked with, where there was always something fun to do, was the last piece of the puzzle, completing the shift back. Life seemed less stressful without class assignments, exams, and deadlines. I had family and friends close by, money in my pocket, and I enjoyed myself. During this time, I began to find a sense of balance and a renewed sense of self, which was crucial as I navigated this new phase of adulthood.

On Friday nights after work, my roommates and I would head to The See-I, a lively spot close to the local college where you could grab a burger and a beer. We also designated Friday night as laundry night because the laundromat was conveniently next door to our hangout, making the chore less mundane. The See-I, adorned with pool tables, a jukebox, and food typical of most college bars in America, was a fun place for students to unwind after a long semester of studies and for recreational sports enthusiasts to relax after a game.

Laundry probably took twice as long this way—running back and forth, often losing track of time. But it was convenient to have washing machines so close to beer and food. This routine of multitasking made our Friday nights enjoyable and efficient, setting the stage for another memorable day: Friday, April 3, 1987.

On that Friday, the usual hustle and bustle of The See-I had an air of anticipation—not really. We played pool, listened to the jukebox, and enjoyed the camaraderie of friends, all while keeping an eye on our laundry next door. Little did I know this Friday would stand out for years to come.

I was enjoying my youth, oblivious to adult problems as we ran back and forth to reload washing machines and transfer clothes to dryers when something unexpected happened. I saw a pretty girl I had met my sophomore year in high school. She was the girl I promised my friend I wouldn't talk to or dance with. And now, she was at the bar. I couldn't help but stare as she walked in with her friends. My taste hadn't changed in six years and I still wanted to talk to her.

As I imagined scenarios where she gave me her number, I started getting nervous. I thought, *I look like crap. How should I approach her? She's not going to like me.* But after a bit, she walked by on her way to the bathroom. A friend noticed my focused interest, smiled at me, and made a cheeky comment. He picked up my beer on his way to her table. Knowing her well, he tried to help, coaxing me to follow.

My heart raced as I approached Sylvia's table, hoping this unexpected encounter would lead to something memorable.

Tony said hi to everyone and her friends made room in the booth for us as I mustered the courage to join them, nervous. We all talked for a few minutes. And while we talked, I became hopeful I would have an opportunity to interact with Sylvia more than just exchanging smiles across the table. Unfortunately, my hope vanished when they told us they were leaving for a nearby city for more action. As they left, I smiled at her and said goodbye, feeling bummed that I would be left to do laundry with my friends, my head hanging in defeat without getting her number. I wished I had been braver and spoken up.

Just three weeks earlier, I'd run into her at a local dance club. She was with her sister when I approached her to dance. But I was turned down and walked away defeated. It seemed I had struck out again, and I wondered if I would ever get another chance.

We spent the rest of the evening at The See-I because we had laundry to finish. I kept thinking about Sylvia and how I had screwed up. Over the next few hours, we made more trips back and forth to finish the laundry, ate dinner, and settled in to enjoy the rest of the night.

Gathered around three or four tables assembled end to end, about 20 of us laughed, listened to music, and enjoyed the 80s in typical fashion. Despite the fun, my mind kept drifting back to Sylvia—how pretty she looked. The evening was winding down as I sat at the end of the group near the entrance, with my back to the door.

I tried to shake off the disappointment and focus on the present moment. The laughter of my friends and the familiar tunes from the jukebox provided a comforting backdrop. But every now and then, I found myself glancing towards the door, hoping for a surprise that might change the course of the evening.

Then, around 11:00, I felt a touch on my shoulder. When I turned around and saw Sylvia, my heart skipped a beat. I asked her where her friends were, and she told me she'd left them to come back. She'd changed her plans for me! Eager for her to be close, I looked around for an available chair, but there wasn't one.

So, with a bit of hope and a smile, I sat back down, moved my knee out, and asked her if she wanted to sit. She smiled back at me and cozied up on my knee. My friends noticed and gave knowing smiles and nods, adding to the happy giddy moment that would forever be remembered.

As we settled in, we talked and laughed, and I felt a sense of contentment and excitement that I hadn't felt in a long time. And the rest, as they say, is history.

It was a long, roundabout way back to her—seeing her six years before, moving away, coming back home, and now finally having her close to me. I remembered the way she looked back then, how she had captured my attention even as a sophomore. Over the years, I had heard about her, but the timing was never right.

Looking back, this moment feels like the culmination of years of hope and longing, finally fulfilled. At the time, I just felt like I got lucky.

Our first date started with lunch purchased at a local market. We agreed to keep it simple—lying on beach towels in the park, covered in coconut oil, basking in the sun. We spent the afternoon eating, talking, laughing, and getting to know each other.

I wasn't exactly sure how she felt. But early during the date, I remember wanting so much to impress her, to get her to like me more than what a first date usually represents. Despite the cliché, I did not want the afternoon to end. We had spent a wonderful afternoon together, or at least I thought we had.

However, I had little faith in relationships. After the date, I was hesitant to share my feelings with anyone. All my friends would have laughed if I had said, "I think she's the one." It was too soon. I worried I might say or do something wrong on our next date. Maybe I was wrong about the whole day being good.

The response for me was to be cautious. I had dated before, but until then, I didn't want to be all in so quickly. Placing all your eggs in one basket can mean losing everything, and I felt vulnerable thinking long term. I didn't want to be hurt. So I tried to dismiss the emotions that kept me on guard to have a chance with her. Despite my trepidation, Sylvia and I quickly grew fond of each other.

As we spent more time together, I noticed how easy it was to talk to her, how her laughter brightened my day, and how comfortable I felt in her presence. The walls were coming down as these moments created hope. Admittedly, I didn't even think in those terms. Hope was for fairytales in books. Instead, I began to have confidence in the future. Maybe taking a risk was worth it. We shared more time together, more laughs, and more conversations that deepened our connection. In the end, I found myself looking forward to our time together, feeling less guarded and more open to the possibilities of what we could become.

Two months after we started dating, I bought Sylvia a beginner set of golf clubs. I loved golf. But it was an odd gift and a little self-serving because I wasn't sure she even liked the sport. Despite her background in sports, limited to drill team and cheering for her wrestling brothers, she was willing anyway. And I hoped she would enjoy golf so we could play together—again, self-serving.

We unpacked her set and went to a local high school, where I taught her how to swing a club, explained the purpose of each club, and shared the basics of the game. And as we did, we laughed and connected, becoming closer. Later, after learning to golf, even when she didn't want to play, Sylvia was a good sport and walked with me, giving me another excuse to hold her hand, kiss her, and talk to her.

I cherished these moments, learning more and more about each other. It wasn't just about golf; it was about sharing experiences, deepening our bond, and discovering new aspects of each other. Wanting a deeper connection was new to me. Sylvia's willingness to join me in this adventure spoke volumes about her supportiveness and our growing connection.

The weeks flew by. And suddenly, Sylvia's birthday—the first we would celebrate as a couple—approached. I found myself in uncharted territory—cautiously hopeful for a memorable celebration. With hope guiding me, I pondered for a long time over ideas to make the day special, still worried about losing. But eventually, I came up with a plan. Everyone loves being sung to. And I adore music and dancing. The only problem? I couldn't sing. However, with karaoke bars popping up everywhere, I settled on the next best thing—lip-syncing a song for her, silly as it may seem.

The first challenge was where to pull off this plan. After a few phone calls, a local restaurant informed me they had a PA system. Excitedly, I reserved their banquet room, and the manager, upon hearing my plans, offered her full support. I also reached out to Sylvia's friends, who eagerly agreed to participate and be there before the big surprise.

Sylvia's birthday was approaching faster than I had expected, leaving me wondering if I had forgotten something—my usual MO. As the day drew nearer, my anticipation and anxiety grew. I imagined her reaction and hoped everything would go off without a hitch.

Thankfully, the support from the restaurant staff and Sylvia's friends reassured me that the surprise would be a success, despite my nerves. Preparing for two weeks, I practiced lip-syncing to Tony Terry's "Forever Yours," smiling and rehearsing with the hope that my effort would show her how romantic I could be.

My plan was to ask Sylvia out for a birthday dinner and suggest a restaurant, having planted a seed during conversations about margaritas and Mexican food. She was delighted and agreed to dine at the place SHE chose, unaware of the surprise I had already arranged at the restaurant.

On the day of her birthday, everything was in place. Hidden in the car were a necklace and a big cheesy teddy bear—the type you win for your girlfriend at the state fair when you're 14. During the long ride there, I kept practicing the song over and over in my head as we drove to the restaurant. The manager had agreed to help covertly retrieve the gifts when Sylvia wasn't looking. Everyone was ready. I was nervous.

Screwing this up and making a fool of myself was something I didn't want to do. More than that, I felt vulnerable. I could lose ground with this tacky display. That would only confirm that I shouldn't take a chance—not go all in—ever.

When we arrived, the manager recognized us from the conversations she and I had and greeted us with a wink when we walked into the restaurant. Wearing a smile, she led us to the back of the restaurant where Sylvia's friends were waiting—Sylvia questioning the walk down the hall.

When we turned the corner into the reserved room, they welcomed us with birthday wishes, rowdy cheers, and thumbs-ups. She was surprised, maybe a bit embarrassed, but generous with a big hug for all the trouble. And for the next hour, we had a good time celebrating her birthday, eating dinner, and laughing. I got to know some of her friends—occasionally receiving a smile conveying their knowledge of my plans.

The stage was set. All the preparation—the calls to the restaurant and Sylvia's friends, hours practicing the song, and successfully keeping the surprise a secret brought us to this moment. Either we grew closer or the over-the-top birthday surprise sent up red flags.

Toward the end of the meal, I managed to sneak away to prepare for the show. With the help of staff behind the scenes, I gathered the gifts, a tall bar stool, and my shaky nerves. Then, our waitress placed the bar stool in the center of the room. And I asked Sylvia to sit, catching her off guard. She was visibly nervous, unsure what came next—with all eyes on her. As she sat in the center of the room, the manager gave me a nod and the rehearsed song began to play on the PA system. And I gave her the gifts. Then, I hammed it up and mouthed the words doing my best to paint a happy memory. Everyone had a good time. Best of all, Sylvia looked at me with an affection I've never felt. I found my way into her heart.

Sylvia and I spent a lot of time together after that. We danced, went to dinner, movies, and sporting events, and hung out with friends and family that winter and spring. I visited her for lunch during her shifts working at a hospital. Our relationship grew as we fell for each other and discussed the future.

The growing relationship felt good for other reasons. We complemented one another, filling the gaps of our weaknesses. I search for solutions when there seem to be none—a veiled idealist. And I procrastinate more than I should.

Sylvia is an introvert, shy, and avoids attention. She might say that she likes flying under the radar. But she can stand her ground if feeling strongly about something. She is also tender, compassionate, capable, and does not procrastinate.

I still had that quiet voice warning me that trouble would eventually come. Trust had always been difficult for me, even when life's events unfolded to suggest otherwise.

I didn't realize that the persistent angst from the challenges I faced growing up was a significant part of my self-sabotage. My biggest flaw—a deeply hidden fear of trust—made me fear commitment and marriage as well. If you trust someone, you'll eventually be let down—or let them down. Yet, despite this fear, I yearned for what others seemed to have—a happy ending.

We married after three years. We were young and passionate, trying to find our way. And we were very much in love. We welcomed our baby Jacob, unaware of all that lay ahead. He was at the center of our existence—more than enough to ground me, to heal a wounded heart.

I loved the idea of being a father and husband. They were beautiful.

But ups and downs that challenge all young couples—lack of experience, immaturity, our past—affected us more than they should. Finances, emotions, and responsibility fueled our arguments. And more often, my inability to expose my weaknesses to anyone who cared about me caused the most concerning issues.

When we started our marriage, I worried about the end, stressed that I wasn't worthy of a family—worthy of Jacob and Sylvia. My faults and decisions would challenge our future and the love we had.

Chapter 3

NOVEMBER 9TH, 1992

Even for Idaho, freezing temperatures, snow, and icy roads at the beginning of November are atypical. In 1992, the sudden cold snap had wreaked havoc on my construction jobs, causing delays and postponements, adding to the list of things in my life unfinished. Juggling several projects, including school, I found myself stretched thin, working late into the afternoon to accommodate the weather-related changes to my schedule.

By the time a few boxes were checked off, the day winding down, I was exhausted. But I still had one last errand: meeting a friend to collect a check for some work I'd done for his business. We had agreed to meet late in the day. And when we finally connected, he offered to buy me dinner at a local sports pub. Starving and worn out, the idea of relaxing over a meal sounded perfect. It also felt like a well-deserved reward for a job well done, a justifiable reason to be out.

The pub was warm and bustling when we arrived at the grill. Brian treated me to a burger and beer and gave me my check. As we chatted about work, our softball team, and the idea of organizing a basketball team—the usual friendly banter—I lost track of time. The food was good, the beer refreshing, and for a moment, my weariness seemed to melt away.

But like the metaphor of the boiling frog, this comfort lulled me into a false sense of security. Later that night, a friend I hadn't seen in a while sent over a large pitcher of beer. Feeling carefree and caught up in the moment, I indulged.

As we sat there eating and drinking, I didn't think about the freezing rain from the previous week or how exhausted I was. And so, irresponsibly, I got in my car and drove away.

Behind the wheel on the freeway, I dozed off and jerked the wheel of my car, continuing the catastrophic chain of events that began when I agreed to dinner and drank a few beers. In an instant, I was sliding sideways on the road, out of control. The tires of my top-heavy vehicle gained traction. And it started tumbling over and over, partially throwing me out and crushing me underneath.

After the crash settled, right before everything turned black, I briefly felt the cold as I lay on my back in the middle of the two-lane freeway. I looked up into the fall night, my body and senses numb. There was no emotion, no comprehension—just night and cold.

My body lay among the scattered remains of the wreck, littering the highway with shattered hopes and an improbable future.

My life was spared because a quick-thinking young man named Eric, who had been driving behind me, witnessed the accident. He immediately stopped his vehicle, parked it across both lanes, and frantically waved off an oncoming 18-wheeler and other vehicles, preventing further tragedy and giving me a chance. Also among the witnesses was Terri, a former EMT, who rushed to the scene to help. Together, they performed CPR until the paramedics arrived.

I had sustained cuts and tears to nerves and flesh, along with many visible broken bones. And when the ambulance crew arrived, they stabilized me as much as possible. However, the paramedics were resigned about the outcome, given the extent of my injuries. Terri, now deeply invested, asked if they would call for air transport. But they said I was unlikely to make it, so the helicopter wasn't called.

Clinging to life, I maintained a heartbeat during my ride to St. Luke's emergency room. At the hospital, I was triaged and immediately sent to surgery, where they used screws, plates, and rods to put me back together. The outlook was grim.

It took a second of poor judgment—a choice that shattered my life into pieces in ways unimaginable.

"Brian, thanks for the check. I'll have to pass on dinner. I'm too tired."

That's what I should have said. Instead, I ruined everything.

Confusion

A few days later, I opened my eyes, unable to focus. The smell of gasoline lingered in the air. And I found myself lying on a hard counter in what seemed like a mechanic shop or garage—my senses betraying me. *Where am I?!* In the distance, I could hear faint sounds—maybe voices. The environment was foreign. Confusion. I felt uneasy, and the beeps, whirs, and strange smells didn't assuage my growing angst. I couldn't think straight.

As my vision became less dreamlike, I noticed the ceiling above me. I tried to turn my head to see more but felt a restraining pressure around my neck from something unfamiliar, hard, and uncomfortable. Glancing around as much as I could, I became frightened when I noticed my feet in strange boots. I was in an inclined bed...

SOMEONE HELP ME! Panic turned to terror when I tried to sit up and couldn't. I tried to move my arms—to move my head—to scream. Nothing happened. GOD HELP ME! Each second brought more fear, and I realized I wasn't breathing normally. My breaths weren't mine and came from a machine next to my bed in a hospital. I was so confused and numb—my head was spinning—thoughts and emotions out of control.

There were so many questions. But I couldn't concentrate on anything other than fear as my mind raced. On the edge of my vision, I noticed my cousin, Rachel, just long enough to see her leave the room before I could say anything. "Please don't leave!"—the voice, only in my head, wasn't heard. I was alone for a moment before Sylvia walked in to replace her.

Her smile was comforting. But I saw sadness in her smile, too. She looked tired, as if she'd been crying, while she kissed my face and reached for my hand. My emotions and senses were out of control. All I could think of as she held my hand to comfort me was that I couldn't feel her touch. I just wanted to close my eyes and wake up from this nightmare.

My memories of an accident were vague. Over the next two days, they told me I had rolled my Jeep. I was partially thrown out of the vehicle during the crash, crushing my body. There were many fractured bones—including several in my cervical column. My spinal cord was damaged. And I was PARALYZED. The awful word carried so much weight when I heard it. A stifling weight that made me want to hide—to escape it.

The news was depressing as they tried to minimize the sting of every medical term or phrase spoken to me after that first conversation. Every smile, every kind word, had little meaning. And I unconsciously began hoping for death, wanting the pain to go away.

When they operated, doctors fused my cervical spine, placed steel rods in my right leg and left arm, and a feeding tube in my stomach. I was fragile but alive. They informed my family about the physical and psychological struggles I would face in the coming weeks. The days would be long and overwhelming as my family and medical staff tried to mitigate the growing sadness they saw in me. Even as I coped, I knew the best-case outcome wasn't me walking out of the hospital. The effort to keep me optimistic was only made more difficult by what I saw in the people I loved.

They constantly reminded me that I was alive and that it was too soon to know anything for sure. Hearing the right words—you have to stay positive and continue to hope because your body could heal and regain some function—didn't help me process any of it. I could see and feel their heartache—especially the sorrow in Sylvia's eyes. Behind her smile and outward strength, I'd hurt and caused her sadness that made me secretly hope for death when I was alone.

Family, friends, and acquaintances came to show their love and support, saying they loved me and were praying for us. Quite a few even moved into a waiting room, ordered pizza, and watched rented movies. However, as nurses, family, and friends became counselors and cheerleaders, trying to lessen our pain, their hope was noise to me. I couldn't escape the obvious—no matter how kind they were. It was too soon to see anything but the storm we were in.

The days blurred together, filled with the sterile smells of the hospital, the constant beeping of monitors, and the soft murmur of concerned voices. And my family's attempts to comfort me only highlighted the gravity of my situation. Sylvia's strength was also a facade. Her eyes betrayed her true feelings. I was alive, but at what cost?

The weight of their sorrow and my uncertain future was unbearable.

I spent the next few weeks recovering from surgery. Time healed my broken bones and my feeding tube was removed after a couple of weeks. But the paralysis made me unable to breathe on my own. I was dependent on a machine to fill my lungs with precious air. If I wanted to live long, I couldn't stay on it.

Weaning off a ventilator is complicated and requires specialized treatment. And St. Luke's Hospital had little experience with this kind of long-term therapy. So, discussions between medical staff and Sylvia resulted in a decision to transfer me to Rancho Los Amigos, a rehab hospital in Downey, California. Rancho was on the cutting edge of spinal cord injury rehabilitation. Craig Hospital in Denver was also a consideration. But since my brother-in-law, Hector, lives in California, it made sense for me to be there.

Added heartbreak—Jacob would stay with the Calsen family while we were away. My son had been part of their daycare since birth, so he was at home with and loved by the Calsens. They had volunteered to watch over him for as long as it took while we focused on the next, forced decision connected to this new reality. We were thankful and broken-hearted because THEY would become his family.

There were fleeting moments when I believed things might get better—moments when a smile or positive word gave me hope. The reality, however, was that passing time only delivered heartache. I was leaving—far away. And I would lose the comfort and solace of being with family and friends. That was terrible enough. Worse, Sylvia and I were leaving. And Jacob would stay behind. Reassuring him that everything would be okay was impossible. I would be gone for a long time, failing my two-year-old son more than I already had.

He was too young to understand this. The anguish and sorrow that we all felt was agonizing.

I had let everyone down, especially Jacob. And the indescribable guilt that consumed me was more than I could handle as I considered the future, waiting for something else I couldn't control. With each new day, life deteriorated

My thoughts were dark, hope depleted, and guilt was all I had left. My mind constantly raced when I was lucid: *You hurt everyone, ruined your life, you should have died.* There was nothing that could soothe me. Only time could heal—or at least mitigate the pain. I didn't think I had much time left.

Chapter 4

Rancho Los Amigos

Sleeping through most of the flight to Rancho Los Amigos was part of an out-of-focus nightmare. The transition from St Luke's to Rancho—the difference between Idaho and California—however, was dramatic and all too real. In 1992, the riots following the Rodney King trial upended parts of the state. The city of Downey—our home now—was at the epicenter of that chaos.

Life continued to unravel for us there as our late afternoon arrival brought me to my room in a half-lucid state. There was no chance to speak to Sylvia during the transfer. Adding to her pain, Sylvia, even though she pleaded, was not allowed to stay that first night in the room with me. She was now alone in a foreign world without family and friends—without Jacob. So, Sylvia cried herself to sleep on a vinyl bench in a waiting room because I couldn't hold her hand, console her, or make eye contact in this unfamiliar place. My desire to make things right—to help her—was replaced by a lonely struggle to make sense of our new surroundings—to pray for death so she could go home.

Our lives had been stripped of everything familiar. The gunshots, helicopters, and mind-numbing disorder provided a steady source of angst and fear in this new location.

The entire time at St. Luke's Hospital in Boise, staff provided blankets and pillows for the family in the waiting room. They made special trips to bring me pizza at midnight. They accommodated every request and concern. They pampered us. Now, we were far from home without anyone to tell us we could get through this. Nothing made sense. There was no way for me to adjust to the stale-smelling room that imprisoned me. Everything—the location, the mood, the air we breathed—seemed to become more difficult to take in with each ticking second. Being at Rancho—surrounded by numbing hospital static—was a sign that I would never be able to help those I love.

Redemption felt impossible.

We had decided to come to California because Sylvia's brother, Hector, lives there—someone available for support. Arranged two weeks before, Sylvia was to stay in a dorm room for students, staff, or patient families visiting the hospital. But walking back to the room alone that first night was scary for her, so Hector came the next day to walk her from my room in the hospital to the dorm she would live in during my rehab. That was solace. Every night for two weeks, Hector escorted Sylvia two hundred yards to make her feel safe. He only stayed long enough to encourage me and walk her home—maybe 20 or 30 minutes. We didn't realize until much later that the round-trip drive took him over three hours.

Sylvia deeply missed Jacob. Being away from him was unbearable. And she also missed home, longing for a past version of life. Rancho was difficult for her without anyone or anything to lift her spirits. And though I never saw her cry, I knew she did.

Adding to the uncertainty, there was no timeline for my treatment, nothing to work toward or hope for. While I questioned my life, she questioned everything too—the dingy room, the violence outside the walls, Jacob's absence, the future—everything. Without a specific plan in place, we began meeting Rancho's staff during the first days. We met nurses, respiratory therapists, and aids.

Early in the morning of the third day, a physical therapist came to assess my paralysis. Maybe I still had hope—the stubborn part of me waited to receive a morsel of something positive. So, when she entered my room, introduced herself, read my chart notes, and checked my range of motion, I paid attention. As part of a test, she asked me to close my eyes while she lifted my arm. But when she asked me to tell her where my arm was in space, I responded and opened my eyes—realizing I was wrong. I became upset and fought back tears. It was another slap in the face, another awful dose of reality.

After Mrs. Graff's arm test, each professional I met brought tests and sobering adjectives that further defined my situation. Meeting a social worker, doctors, more therapists, and CNAs over the next few days only added to my angst—more hard truths.

A few days later, after adjusting a bit to a schedule, I awoke to an overhead light and stirring in my room. Usually, I was bathed at 5:00 a.m. (oddly with cold water) and clothed. I also had my medicine dispensed and my vent checked at this time. Sometimes, I slept through the commotion, tired from restless nights and monotonous routines. But most of the time, I was awakened by the disruptions.

The activity was remarkable on this day. After an anonymous staff member entered my room—staying only a second to disturb me—I was left alone, hoping to fall asleep again. During the disturbance, I hadn't even opened my eyes. This morning was different because bathing hadn't started immediately after my wake-up routine.

Following the interruption, as the seconds passed and I hovered in a half-awake state, I realized my breathing was different. Suddenly wide awake with fear, I opened my eyes, waiting for the next breath from my ventilator. But it took longer than usual. Something was definitely wrong. My mind began racing. The lapse between breaths was noticeably longer, enough for me to count the seconds in my head. A few more delayed breaths passed, and panic took over as my oxygen saturation dropped and my body needed more air.

It was a familiar, dreadful script of fear and anxiety. Just days before, I had playfully learned to whistle without the vent, finding humor in the process. But now, it was my only option. Desperately, I started whistling as loudly as possible to alert someone.

As if the fear wasn't enough, the situation revealed a vulnerability I didn't think was possible—I felt more exposed, more fragile than yesterday! My lungs were filling less. And I was alone. A minute, maybe two, passed. It seemed MUCH longer. Then, hearing my repeated chirps, one of my daily nurses, starting her morning shift, rushed into the room. Skilled at her job, she quickly noticed my gasps for extra breaths, my panic, and adjusted the ventilator. As she returned the machine to its previous settings, she saw my emotion.

"Don't worry," she said.

Unsettled, I thought, *What the hell is going on?* My nurse had corrected the obvious error and calmed me down a bit. But WHAT

THE HELL!!! As she left the room, she reassured me that she would find out what happened. Then I was alone again. Two or three more minutes passed as my imagination got the best of me. During the painful anxious wait, my doubts, confusion, and anger turned into despair when an unknown respiratory therapist poked her face past the semi-closed door and apologized.

"Sorry, wrong room," she muttered, and then left.

Now I was angry. How could this happen? I wanted to scream at someone, to let them know that I was hurting.

My nurse returned after five minutes and informed me of what I already knew. A respiratory therapist I had not seen before had mistakenly changed the output of my ventilator from 12 breaths—one breath every five seconds—to six breaths—one breath every 10 seconds. I'm not sure if I would have succumbed to this stupid mistake, although someone had passed a few months earlier due to another ventilator mishap. But this blunder stole the last bit of hope I had. With a small slip, all the doubts and fears I had set aside returned to the surface.

A few days later, I asked a doctor about my prognosis. His callous dismissal of my anxiety and fear was like a kick to the face when I was already down. His response was the final straw. I was lost. Constantly feeling a glimmer of hope only to have it snatched away had taken its toll. I no longer wanted to trust. I couldn't breathe deeply anymore. Waiting for the next terrible thing to happen, I was barely hanging on.

Good people kept us afloat when we least expected it. Another patient's wife befriended Sylvia during the first week in the dorms.

Shortly after learning about our situation, this stranger approached Sylvia and said she wanted to do something for us. Monica and Roy made the incredible gesture of flying my parents and Jacob to Rancho for Christmas. Their kind, selfless act was a lifeline. Others also kept us from giving up by offering an encouraging word or a kind smile. However, so much was unfairly tipping the scale that, after Jacob and my parents left that weekend, the days continued to move painfully slowly.

The acts of compassion became lost in the sadness of an uncertain future. And we settled back into an uncomfortable depression. A week later, a test to determine if I would breathe again revealed that my diaphragm wasn't working. And they told us that my phrenic nerve was severed. I would remain on a ventilator for the rest of my life. The verdict erased all hope for the future.

Yet persistence—the kind of internal determination that subconsciously searches for distractions, reasons to find something positive, a ray of light in the darkness—seemed present in my fight. I grasped for anything that might help me feel better.

Sunday church service, even though it was held in a converted room at Rancho, felt like an escape from the cold rooms and lousy food. A few weeks in, a small group of us began attending, searching for answers in a place filled with bitter fruit. For others, it was just a break from monotony.

One Sunday, a vent patient named Mario was ushered to the front so he would be out of the way. Along with staff, patients, and a few others in the converted room, a mother and her two small children sat behind Mario before church began. During the sermon, I tried to focus on the pastor's message, hoping for some encouragement. But for some reason, the two toddlers held my attention more than the chaplain's words. In their defense, the service was usually bland—a regular sermon for those lost and confused about having been dealt a blow. So, the youthful energy of children was more interesting to me that morning.

Suddenly, as I smiled at their exuberance, a loud, obnoxious alarm pierced the room, signaling something was wrong with a ventilator. At that moment, Mario stopped breathing.

Now I can't explain why part of me wanted to laugh as I watched the mother snatch the tube from her toddler son, then frantically try to figure out where it belonged. I knew it was heartless to react that way. Maybe I needed a laugh, a distraction from the general gloom of this place. The incident seemed rehearsed and comedic, like an episode of *I Love Lucy* as she frantically poked around to fix her toddler's mistake.

Someone intervened after 15 or 20 seconds. And the vent started providing air for Mario again—relief. It wasn't a very traumatic mishap. But it certainly affected him. Unfortunately, a bit paranoid of little children near his vent, he never returned to church again.

In retrospect, finding humor in the incident, given my own vent mistake and the terror I had experienced, was paradoxical. But when you're wading through quicksand, you will reach for anything to free yourself. So, as cringe-worthy as it was, I found it funny—laughing as loud as my vent-filled lungs allowed.

In the days that followed, I witnessed a fellow patient experience a choking incident, relentless nighttime disruptions from patients, and staff performing their duties at all hours of the day and night. I was also privy to disheartening stories of others like me. The volume of disorder within the day was so consuming and depressing that it was hard to imagine a future or anything beyond the walls of Rancho.

When I met Irma, I was the lowest I had ever been. I concluded, through all the pain, that signs from God revealed I was a terrible person who deserved this. I didn't think I had anything left. Irma was one of several respiratory therapists assigned to our ward. Others rotated through. But they hadn't made a notable impression. No one had. Instead, the focus of my conscious, minute-to-minute thoughts wrestled with phantom pain, my paralysis, and everything negative at Rancho Los Amigos.

I was still angry about the vent mistake when she walked in that morning. Unable to speak, I responded to her presence with a suspicious look and an angry headshake—trying to convey distrust the only way I could. She probably didn't know about the ventilator mistake or anything else about me—other than what my chart said. However, her calm response to my overreaction was the beginning of something I didn't expect.

The distress I expressed as she walked toward my life-giving machine prompted an unusual reaction from her.

"It's going to be okay," she said.

Bitter, scared, and defeated, I didn't want to hear it! And I angrily shook my head again in disapproval. How could she know anything about me? I was not okay! I glared at her as she smiled—my defenses pushing back. As she moved about the room—and I watched her every move—she took a minute between checking my settings and checking on me.

"I know you're worried and scared," she said. The acknowledgment was enough for me to focus on her voice—her spirit disarming despite my angry internal objection. Her demeanor quelled the exasperation in me. Why was she doing this? I was just another of hundreds of people she had looked after. I was not special. Rancho and everything there was stale, cold, and reminiscent of tragedy. I didn't trust her. Then, Irma paused and planted an out-of-place seed of hope.

She said, "I want you to take all your worries, fears, and doubts and put them in a box. Then, I want you to give them to God." Guarded, I thought to myself, who does she think she is?

I'd heard these words in church before this time. Since adolescence, I've always held uncertainty about much of it. Specific memories from the first six years of a scary childhood and being worried reinforced mistrust—memories that I learned later in life weren't typical.

I trusted very little growing up. And I didn't trust anyone at Rancho. I did not want to trust Irma. Yet how she talked to me felt different from others I'd already met. She lacked indifference and apathy. Despite the never-ending carousel of spinal cord injuries and the dejected patients whose lives were changed, Irma remained positive. She showed kindness and care. Irma didn't say much else while finishing the ventilator check. But before she left, she said one more thing.

"I want to help you."

During the next week, Irma checked my vent daily and asked yes or no questions about my life as I nodded to communicate. Her gentle and kind approach broke down the walls I'd created to protect myself. As she broke down my guard, she built trust—opening a door I'd closed a while back. I didn't realize she was leading me by hand so I could hope for the impossible. So I could believe it WAS possible. For some reason, Irma chose to do something for ME, something that could have cost her job. And it wasn't long before she told us her plan.

She said, "I want to get you off the vent."

Her statement was very matter of fact and we were surprised by her conviction. We reminded her that my diaphragm no longer worked. And that the doctor, over a week before, informed us that I would forever be dependent on my ventilator. Despite that, wearing this soft, comfortable tenderness, Irma continued to present her case.

She said, "Doctors don't know everything. I want to help you. But you need to trust me." She was asking us to believe that our doctors could be wrong—that we could have faith. The expressions on our faces revealed our doubt.

"It will not be easy. And you will have to work hard, but I want to help you," she repeated.

There had been so much pain and disappointment during the last three months. Here was someone else trying to keep us from losing the battle. Even though it felt like grasping at straws, it sounded like a possibility coming from her.

Irma came to the hospital early the following Saturday morning. She wasn't officially working. She even brought us a meal from home to put me at ease. Our connection to her felt different this day—different than a typical patient and therapist interaction. She made small talk. But I understood she wanted to get to work by the ambiguity of the conversation. After the chit-chat, she transitioned into her instruction.

First, she explained that she would turn off my machine and remove the tube connected to my tracheostomy. Soberly, she said I would have to focus on breathing. I had to imagine my lungs filling with air—to imagine using my body even though I couldn't, even though it felt impossible. She failed to mention how terrifying it would be. As she explained, Sylvia and my brother, Ray, who arrived a week after us, encouraged me. Still, I felt a bit scared as she moved over to the machine and turned it off.

I didn't understand that so much of the future depended on this moment. Whether I lived a long, productive life or passed from pneumonia in six years depended on how I would manage my fears, expectations, and my will to see a possible future.

As she removed the tube from the plastic trachea in my throat, the same rush of emotion I experienced after waking up the week of my accident enveloped me like a cold, freezing blanket. I became acutely aware that my chest stopped moving. And that the mechanical push of air was no longer audible. I felt panic—like someone was trying to end me, as I violently shook my head—trying to take in the life-sustaining oxygen needed to live. It was impossible to focus on their voices as I fought to breathe. Self-preservation, the innate reflex, kept me from rational thought. It seemed like an eternity as I struggled unsuccessfully.

My time off the vent was only a couple of tear-filled minutes of terror before I started desaturating. Irma was ready, connecting me back to my ventilator as my vision narrowed and my hearing turned into a high-pitched ring.

These attempts at weaning happened five or six times a week for two weeks. Each time we tried, I failed. After a while, it wasn't the fear of being taken off the vent that concerned me the most. I had learned how to suppress the innate fight for life with a more focused effort. But I worried about what would happen if none of this worked.

You can't nurture hope and doubt at the same time. You just can't.

Each time I failed to breathe, more doubt grew.

Two Saturdays later, a group gathered in my room. The weekly rendezvous sometimes involved several people. Perhaps my brother's humor attracted staff and patients to our room. Or the different personalities provided the right mix of characters to create an environment dissimilar to a hospital one—an escape. Either way, we had frequent weekend visitors—the usual posse there to listen to Hector give a brief, 15-minute Saturday morning sermon. It was nice to get a pick-me-up after the week's lunacy. After each speech, everyone talked, laughed, and visited while I felt less like a patient and more like the host of a party.

Sometime during their visit, as they helped bring normalcy to the week, I realized something was wrong. No one noticed I was having difficulty breathing. Self-consciousness prevented me from shaking my head to alert someone. I didn't want to make a scene. But I had to get their attention. It was puzzling, though, when the mood in the room didn't change after they noticed me making strange head gestures to prevent another vent mishap. Some even wore grins.

Then, Irma interjected. Smiling, she looked at me and said, "You've been off the ventilator for a while." Apparently, during the visit, Irma had turned off my vent while I focused on the activity in the room. There was no chance to react to the angst of being removed from the ventilator. And for three minutes, unaware, I'd created enough movement to oxygenate my body. I breathed without a vent! Everyone knew what she'd done. Their indifference during my confusion—and a warm laugh after she told me—finally made sense.

The revelation changed expectations as Irma, Sylvia, and my brother continued disconnecting me from the ventilator. Following my success, Irma ramped up her efforts to motivate me—sometimes dangling a carrot to keep me focused. I didn't need the push because the possibility of living a vent-free life was enough reason. But she was determined to get me across the line. So, if I achieved a time goal, Irma brought us a home-cooked meal or a pastry she made. The persuasion was the cherry on top as we focused on possibly going home without the added stress of a ventilator. We felt hope. Irma unknowingly and profoundly changed our future and our perspective. With more work, three minutes became five. Then, Irma told us to speak with the doctor.

Dr. Rosencranz was reluctant when Sylvia approached him about my breathing without a ventilator. More than that, he was condescending—slowly explaining, like a teacher to a kindergartener, that tests revealed I needed one. Maybe he was jaded by a long career or didn't care. Either way, he just wanted to dismiss her. During the conversation, my brother turned my ventilator off to prove to him that I could breathe. And the doctor turned to witness my inevitable failure. After watching me struggle to breathe for five minutes, he just walked away—perhaps because he had been proven wrong. There was no encouragement or admonishment—nothing. We were a bit confused, even a little angry, because he controlled my future. However, they told us during the next respiratory therapy visit that Dr. Rosencranz had prescribed to wean me off the vent. It was such an odd, awkward, and pivotal interaction—a decision that changed the course of the next few weeks.

Finally, I could breathe without a vent—a glimmer of something good. The medical team moved me to a room with three other patients who were in the same stage of recovery. The move was positive as it represented progress. But it also felt like a lateral move with many new difficulties. There were constant interruptions in the new chaotic environment. Four patients and the healthcare workers necessary to meet their demands made privacy impossible—and sleep a luxury. Here, nightfall brought its own special misery. Even though I could quell my demons, at times, others often couldn't. They often expressed their despair late into the morning—screaming at the heavens for nurses and at themselves. Ironically, this new room felt more isolated even with more people in it.

Still, I grew stronger. I only used the ventilator at night. But two ventilators in the room added to the cacophony of annoyances and prevented restful sleep.

Also, one of the regular nighttime disturbances occurred when the respiratory therapists came to check the vents at 2:00 a.m. The therapists ensured our machines had enough water and were at the right temperature—humidified air is essential for patient comfort and to prevent other medical issues. The respiratory therapists were quiet. But they often made small talk if they thought we were awake. Is the vent warm enough for you? Is there anything I can do for you?

I was usually awake. But I could only smile at them—unable to use my voice.

A month into my hospital stay, a nighttime respiratory therapist I didn't recognize came to check my ventilator at the usual 2:00 a.m. rouse. My bed was nearest the door, close to the hall light, so I was awake when he glanced at me and whispered, "Bro, I didn't know you were here!" I was confused. I usually recognized the respiratory therapists even though they regularly wore face masks, but I didn't know him.

"What happened, bro? Are you okay?" he asked. I nodded yes to acknowledge that I understood him—still confused.

His demeanor didn't fit the typical vent respiratory therapist approach. He paused, then looked at me and shook his head as if to say he was sorry. Then he continued.

"Remember that little kid that hung out with us in front of that little store? What was his name?" he mumbled to himself. "Does your family still live there?" It was now apparent he thought I was a childhood friend. He continued to make small talk like we were catching up after years of not seeing each other.

"Anyway, bro, I left the neighborhood to live with my grandma. Then, when my son was born, I had to do something. So I went to school. I couldn't stay back there. You know how it is—all the trouble—and I didn't want my son to be in all that." He talked more about characters from the past and about the store where *we* would hang out because we knew the owner.

It was a surreal conversation, familiar and heartwarming. He talked to me like a big brother. He knew I couldn't speak, so his questions were rhetorical. And although it was one-sided, I started feeling like I really knew him. When he finished with our vents, he told me he had to finish his shift and that he was assigned to my building for two weeks.

"Someone was sick or something, so I'll be back," he said. He asked if I needed anything, and I shook my head no. Before he walked away, he grabbed a Snickers from his pocket, placed it on my hospital food table, and told me he was sorry I was there.

His kindness and empathy were authentic. Afterward, I wondered who I reminded him of and thought about the neighborhood and everything he spoke about. For two weeks, he brought me yogurt, candy, and memories belonging to someone else. I didn't try to correct this mistaken identity. It would have been too difficult to explain. And to be honest, I looked forward to his visits as I imagined myself belonging to the memories of the walking, talking person he mistook me for.

As my world continued to change, there were other encouraging boosts to my morale. When I began working with Irma, she introduced me to a PassyMuir valve, a plastic, one-way device that forced air over my vocal cords instead of through the tubing connected to my ventilator. With it in place, I could speak again. This simple device restored my sense of self—at least a little. Being able to communicate, rather than just making muffled sounds, was a big step forward.

Breathing and talking became positive milestones, and I clung to these small victories as I faced three more monotonous weeks in the hospital.

In March, the medical team discussed the possibility of my release. The goal of therapy at Rancho Los Amigos was to prepare us for a life of disability, ideally without the ventilator. To that end, therapists began emphasizing the importance of hydration, nutrition, and mental well-being for maintaining good health. They also instructed me on preventing skin breakdown and managing overheating. In preparation for life after Rancho, I was measured for a quilted abdominal binder to support my back and stomach. And they also provided me with a shower sling, a transfer sling, and a comprehensive three-ring binder filled with information on living as a quadriplegic. It seemed there might finally be an end in sight to my time at Rancho.

Sylvia was home with Jacob while we discussed our options for leaving the hospital. She had returned a month earlier, unable to stay away from him. And her job had called her back as well.

Everything suddenly felt very real. I was excited to go home but anxious about the unknowns, especially regarding the ventilator. After discussing my concerns with a sympathetic nurse named Timoku, she offered to stay overnight to help ease my fear of dying in my sleep without the vent—since that was the next step.

Two days before Sylvia was due back at Rancho, Timoku sat at my bedside. My goal was to fall asleep without my ventilator. Yet my emotions oscillated between the confusion and heartache of Rancho and the anxiety about the future for me and my family. The thought of continuing with the ventilator was almost as overwhelming as the joy of going home. My mind was so active that I stayed up all night, unable to quiet my thoughts. Although disappointed by my sleepless night, Timoku reassured me she would return the following night to try again.

The prospect of leaving the routines I'd grown accustomed to, the mental preparation for going home, and the fear of potentially dying in my sleep had all contributed to my sleeplessness. The implications of either keeping or not keeping the ventilator were huge and depended on whether I could sleep without it.

The following night, exhausted, I fell asleep. When I woke up seven hours later, Timoku was there to greet me.

"See, you're still alive," she said with a reassuring tone. I felt like I had passed a significant test, even as I faced the uncertainty of the new life ahead.

After spending so much time in the rooms and hallways of Rancho, leaving felt like a daunting prospect. I had become strangely dependent on the familiar routines and the emotional comfort they provided. Preparing mentally to leave this place proved challenging and isolating. My reliance on the nurses, aides, and fellow patients caused confusion and angst, making me question the urgency of returning home.

But the doctors had decided. I was ready to be released.

Chapter 5

Coming Home

Preparing to fly home from Rancho was daunting in every sense. Beyond the fear of the plane crashing and the possibility of being trapped in the wreckage, I felt I was returning home a changed person, stripped of my former self. We were going back to see family, but I was now frail and broken. The person they knew was gone, replaced by someone who felt disconnected from his own life—my body and mind were altered, leaving me uncertain about navigating a world that now felt unwelcoming.

The logistics of travel for a quad are involved and often complicated. So, Sylvia, my physical therapist Cindy, and I traveled from the hospital to the airport by special transport. Cindy, who could transfer me from a wheelchair to an airplane seat and back, was a comforting presence, given the angst I felt. Her familiarity was a link to my supportive network of helpers, nurses, and therapists. Being with Sylvia again was reassuring, but I was also anxious about our evolving relationship. From her perspective, the future seemed bleak, though I could sense her determination to get us home and start the next chapter of our lives, whatever it might hold.

Our return home was nothing like we had envisioned. The memories of our former life felt distant and disconnected from the reality we faced.

The thought of confronting this new truth with family and Jacob present, after months of separation, was overwhelming.

I felt incomplete, unable to fulfill the roles and responsibilities that once defined me as a father. The idea of Jacob seeing me differently filled me with despair, and the anticipation of reuniting with my family brought a flood of emotions I had been suppressing.

Upon arriving at Logan Park, the assisted living apartment complex where we would reside temporarily, the angst, worry, and fear made me want to run away. I was good at that. Still, a part of me clung to optimism, yearning for home. Despite the discomfort of the flight with all the wheelchair transfers, and the emotion involved, our lives had to move forward.

Entering through a semi-private entrance, I could hear the commotion as Cindy wheeled me toward the small apartment. We paused at the door, reflecting on the past four months spent in medical and therapeutic settings. The apartment door symbolized a transition from a place of sorrow to one filled with family and old memories.

As we stepped inside, time seemed to slow. Cindy pushed my manual wheelchair—and I wished for a muted welcome with all eyes on Sylvia and not me. But in a rush, our family approached us, embracing and crying, their emotions overwhelming us after our long separation. The sight of them, their heartfelt welcome, and the blending of tenderness and tears was both heartwarming and disorienting.

Sylvia then gathered Jacob and brought him close. This I was unable to prepare for, and I began sobbing uncontrollably. At 3 years old,

Jacob didn't fully grasp what was happening. I had to explain that these were happy tears, even though I was overwhelmed with many different emotions. As we held each other tightly, it was the beginning of a hopeful start.

Understanding the long, emotional day, no one stayed long. Their love had welcomed us into our new life, but we needed to begin healing on our own. So, after everyone left, Sylvia used a Hoyer lift to transfer me from my chair to bed, starting what would become an intricate daily routine. She checked my tracheostomy tube, an irritating reminder of my fragile lungs, administered my medications, and then tucked Jacob in.

Exhausted, Sylvia brushed her teeth and prepared for bed. And as she turned off the lights, darkness and silence enveloped the room. We were alone. The next day marked the beginning of an uncertain future. We faced our new reality alone. There were no doctors, nurses, therapists, or aides to check on us. I didn't have a call switch for emergencies.

The thought of our isolation filled me with dread about our chances for success. But I kept my worries to myself. I had to be strong.

Spring at Logan Park, 1993

At Logan Park, each day felt like nails scraping across a chalkboard—a mix of smiles and discomfort. I battled pneumonia throughout the first year, my lungs frequently needing suction, and the maintenance of my tracheostomy was a constant challenge.

Yet there were moments of joy: Jacob wanted to help and learned to carefully remove and rinse the inner cannula of my trachea himself. Conversely, the daily routine was monotonous and often torturous:

wake up, bathe in bed, dress, take medications, transfer to a chair, eat, watch TV, go back to bed, and repeat.

Despite the bleak routine, seeing Jacob play and laugh was a bright spot. Consequently, life had become a series of good and bad, revealing the irony that to appreciate life, we often need to face struggle.

I was coping with my new disability, but so were Sylvia and Jacob. Sylvia was overwhelmed by the unexpected burdens. Jacob's hopeful words, "When you feel better, Dad, we can go outside and play," were both heartwarming and heartbreaking. His impossible hope reminded me of everything we had lost.

Also, Sylvia and I had obstacles of our own. We had to rekindle what had been lost. We were still the same people but had been changed by recent months. We couldn't fully appreciate the small successes yet. The gains seemed fleeting amid our unfamiliar and uncertain lives. And they didn't address our relationship anyway. We could have used counseling. But with so many people in and out of our small apartment, I didn't want to add to the chaos. Instead, we leaned on our large families and faith.

Our routine was also different than I imagined. Jacob spent his weekdays at Abuela Jeanette's because I couldn't care for him. There, he could play with other kids in a warm, loving environment—a comforting solace through our challenges. Sylvia went to work. And I stayed behind, further defining my new station in life. The months dragged on as we all adjusted. I was only faintly aware of a distant glimmer of hope in the darkness.

In the following weeks of monotony, we started receiving visits from nurses, therapists, and other professionals who came to check on our progress. "How are you feeling today? How are your lungs and skin? Are you taking your medications?" they would ask. Their kindness and support were invaluable, especially from my daily caregivers. But their visits were just another part of the noise.

GEORGE

I first met George Hage, an occupational therapist, on the day he came to our apartment to assess my situation. He had been at my bedside a few days after my accident. It had been too soon for anything more than brief conversations with physicians and Sylvia about my condition. Now, months later, George arrived at the senior facility to evaluate my progress.

During our initial conversation, he inquired about my family and interests and spoke warmly about the kindness he had felt during his first assessment in November. His informal approach made me feel like I had known him forever, and I began to let my guard down, much like I had with Irma at Rancho.

Though I was unfamiliar with the detailed role of an occupational therapist, I knew George would help assess my health, deficits, and the obstacles I faced. However, when he shifted to discussing the practical tools he had brought to help me navigate my environment, it hit me hard.

Among the items he presented were mouth sticks—tools for individuals with motor function issues, like quadriplegics, to type and write. The mouth stick, a Y-shaped plastic piece attached to aluminum tubing with a nut for holding a pen or pencil, felt like a slap to the face. Along with them, George gave me a small, hand-crafted easel he had made for their use. I should have felt grateful for these thoughtful gifts, but they symbolized something too stark and permanent for me to embrace with joy. They represented my new reality—DISABILITY. I would have to use my mouth, not my hands, to accomplish tasks. The reality of this tore at my heart, and it ached with the weight of it.

Despite how much reality hurt, George's kindness eased the blow. He could have offered me anything, even an old shoe, and I would have accepted it.

When Jacob saw George place the mouth stick and learned how it could help me, he was eager to help. George handed him a mouth stick and showed him how to offer it to me. And as Jacob climbed next to me in bed and shoved the mouth stick into my mouth, he pressed too firmly and too far back. I gagged, coughed, and my eyes watered for a few minutes. Jacob was surprised and confused—he had only wanted to help.

I didn't want him to feel bad. So, after catching my breath, I gently explained that he needed to be more careful with his Pops.

A few days later, while Jacob and I were sitting next to each other—him on Sylvia's bed next to mine, watching TV, he leaned over and bit my arm hard enough to break the skin. I barely noticed it, adding to his confusion. From my perspective, he was trying to make sense of my condition in his 3-year-old way—my need for help with everything, my brokenness front and center. When he realized what he'd done, tears welled up in his eyes. He understood that he had hurt me because another child bit him at daycare a week before. The last thing he wanted was to hurt me.

Sylvia comforted him, her heart breaking along with his as he wrestled with the emotion. Jacob's attempts to understand my disability led him to test its limits in his own way. And the gifts George had brought intertwined with Jacob's understanding of my condition and our shared past, causing joy and pain.

Mouth Sticks & Coincidence

Years before my injury, our youth group had listened to Joni Eareckson Tada, an inspirational speaker, during an outing aimed at reminding us of gratitude. This amazing woman shared to a full venue how a diving accident had transformed her life and how her faith and determination led her to paint with her mouth. Although the speech was but an instant of my life, her courage left a lasting impression on me.

When George set up my easel and I wrote my name with the mouth stick, we couldn't help but smile. George then revealed that he had been part of the team responsible for bringing Joni to Idaho to speak at the very event our youth group had attended. When I mentioned that I had been in the audience, we shared a "what the heck" moment, laughing at the coincidence—the timing and relationship feeling contrived.

George, purposely or not, provided a means to move forward for me. Drawing became a small way to break the monotony of my days—a way to escape my disability for minutes at a time. And though I didn't expect much from my initial scribbles, engaging in something other than watching television was a welcome change.

Each day with Sylvia, Jacob, and the support from family and friends slowly restored some hope in my life. But progress was slow. And gazing out the window—reliving the past—was counterproductive. I struggled with the stages of loss and was often stuck, unable to envision the future, even with the stints of doodling that sometimes distracted me.

Despite the small victories and distractions, time seemed to crawl.

Greg and Scott, two college friends from Caldwell who were part of my life before Sylvia, came to visit before anyone outside my immediate family had. They were part of a tight-knit group that spent their summers hanging out, floating the river, and playing city league softball. Their visit in the spring of 1993 came at a time when I was wrestling with guilt, sorrow, and a flood of confused emotions. When they surprised me, I knew their visit would be awkward for them. But their familiar smiles and casual demeanor were comforting. So I tried to act normal, though I was uncertain what that meant now as a quadriplegic.

Greg and Scott had to navigate the delicate balance of offering comfort without knowing what to expect. Despair, anger, or even forced positivity could be the reaction they encountered.

That day, the conversation began with the typical dude greetings: "How are you doing, buddy? How are Jacob and Sylvia?" Their effort to treat me like before the accident meant a lot, even though

I felt like I was in a fishbowl. The accident was still fresh in my mind, and their encouragements during the conversation were like words bereft of meaning to my insecurities. The realization of my new reality—my inability to walk and do the things I once took for granted—was overwhelming.

They brought well wishes from other friends. And made more small talk. However, when one of them finally spoke to my disability and said, "Life sucks sometimes," I responded without thinking, "I'm guilty for all of this, for the mistake I made." I felt a deep sense of remorse and a desire to disappear. Scott quickly threw me a lifeline, saying, "You didn't ask for this." His words were a comfort, and Greg added, "We've all done stupid crap before. It's not your fault this happened. It could have happened to any of us." Their response was also an assault to my reality. It wasn't pity. Rather, a lifeline. Words that made sense. Their support, coming from friends rather than therapists or family, felt profoundly meaningful. They reminded me that I could acknowledge my mistakes without losing myself in them.

Their visit was brief after that—maybe 15 or 20 minutes. But it provided the encouragement I needed and meant more to me than they realized.

In the following days, my firefighting friends, Al and Gilbert, visited, giving me further reasons to stay positive. Friends from school, along with my siblings, parents, cousins, and in-laws, continued to offer support. And each visit helped lessen the weight of self-blame. I was learning to draw, finding new distractions, and gradually adapting to my new reality. Though time moved slowly, the ups and downs became less extreme, and the days felt a bit more bearable—bearable to a degree.

Spending most of the day in bed felt like a prison sentence—without a way to shake the guilt that weighed more than the small advances. My mind needed engagement to feel normal, but I often got lost in thoughts about the setbacks we faced. Unable to walk, exercise, or stretch to reset like before, I was overwhelmed.

My understanding of the psychology of loss, learned in college, didn't fully prepare me for applying it to my life. Still, knowing the stages of recovery helped me navigate them—consolation.

Weeks passed as I remained stuck in self-critical thoughts, trying to maintain optimism while managing internal emotions. Everyone, including Sylvia and Jacob, was dealing with their own struggles. Sylvia would sometimes question everything and cry, while Jacob's impossible hopes about the future showed his own confusion. Yet Jacob's need for me—his reminder that I could still be his daddy—served as a catalyst for a glimmer of a NEW perspective on my role and our future. The ups and downs incrementally became less extreme, and the tired days continued improving slightly.

Late in the summer, after Jacob's nudge, I went to Elks Rehab Hospital for a check-up of my tracheostomy and my overall health. The bothersome tube fostered infection. And it was embarrassing to have people stare. I was excited at the thought of having it removed. But I was also nervous about removing it, still mentally dependent. Easing my concern, they explained that the procedure was simple: slide out the plastic cannula, cover the hole with a band-aid, and let it close over in a few days. No longer needing the tracheostomy valve and the relief of not having people stare at my neck or have the Passy valve pop off mid-sentence was emotional. So, after the doctor determined my overall health was stable, he decided it was time to remove the tracheostomy tube. It healed like they said it would. And just as quickly, the symbolic anchor of the plastic tube was gone forever.

Though I no longer needed the vent and my general health improved, my self-image had been altered. I was embarrassed by my frail, atrophied body. Exercise and sports, once sources of confidence, were no longer part of my identity. Since the accident, I often dreamt of exercising, adding to my internal conflict. Despite this, I held on to the belief that life was worth fighting for. Besides, life was getting better.

Chapter 6

Logan Park

The assisted living complex embraced us after I came home broken. We were the only young family in a facility filled with seniors who seemed to crave the presence of youth like an elixir. Over time, everyone and everything there helped make our situation more bearable. The Pinochle ladies loved having a curious little boy full of personality around. They added themselves to his growing list of friendly cheek-squeezers, soaking up his youthful energy. Even movie nights with the residents became a regular event for Jacob, giving him a unique childhood experience.

Logan Park offered amenities few 3-year-olds ever get. Jacob took pride in his unique living situation, telling his daycare friends that he had a cafeteria at home where he could get cookies and juice whenever he wanted. This made him the envy of his little group. For Sylvia and me, our days and weeks revolved around Jacob and his happiness. Watching him adapt to our new reality, as children often do, gave us something to hold on to. We fed off his resilience.

Sylvia was managing that spring and summer. Though her struggles were different, her roles as a loving mom and supportive partner kept her from focusing too much on our unusual living arrangement. But seeing me in pain every day, with no end in sight, was especially hard on her. She knew I would never be the same, and she processed my emotions—worry, sadness, and doubt—while grappling with her own. The extremes of our situation continued the strain of our relationship.

I couldn't help her with many of the responsibilities because I was still figuring out how to live in this new reality. As I clung to any sense of normalcy, Sylvia juggled a job, motherhood, caregiving, advocacy, and emotional support—on her own. This paralyzed life overwhelmed her too. So I made it my focus to be there for her in whatever ways I could, especially as it became clear that our stay at Logan Park would last.

I was drained, emotionally and physically. Each time I smiled to reassure my family, I relived the moment I lost the ability to be whole—to be the partner who fixes things, takes on the load, or acts as the protective husband and father. The burden Sylvia carried was unfathomable, and my attempts to comfort her fell short.

For a relationship to work, there must be balance, a give and take—reciprocal. But during that year, Sylvia was carrying more than her share.

We were treading water, just trying to stay afloat.

We stumbled into a wearisome fall, trying to pretend we were okay. Without the tracheostomy, I felt better. Thanksgiving and Christmas with family—reminders that we should be thankful—were reasons to celebrate life. Our relatives were a consistent part of our progress. Listening to my cousin Mike and his friend Tracy sing in our apartment and watching Jacob play video games with my brother helped move the needle that fall. So did Sylvia's sisters and brothers and friends. They kept us from losing ground.

However, the motions we were going through, the visits and what seemed like filler to keep us above water, felt insincere. I kept telling myself I was alive for a reason. I held on to that when I peered through the bars on my window.

While I tried not living in the past, I often had strange dreams. Sometimes I could fly and see the countryside like a bird. Or I was stranded somewhere with just a towel, trying to hide from a crowd. Sometimes I would go for a drive. Lack of sensory input—unable to feel the world around me while confined to a broken body—created a defense mechanism response. Or perhaps my mind needed an escape of sorts, free from anything traumatic. Either way, a psychiatrist would have had a field day trying to make sense of me.

While I learned to draw with a charcoal pencil in my mouth, I navigated the emotional and psychological challenges—desperate for anything that made me feel better. Using up hours of uninteresting days practicing holding my breath to remain steady and holding the mouth stick to create different angles for the pencil felt productive. Following sports and listening to music to soothe my soul also made me feel better. They were activities that I didn't have to be able-bodied to do. And that felt normal.

Because Sylvia was working again, she had friendship, support, and routines that were familiar. Jacob loved his daycare with his friends and the loving caregivers he saw every day. The innocence and resilience that all children have sustained him. I sat in my wheelchair more. And I ventured outside to spend more time with them. I still wrestled with my emotions, yet seeing them happy was solace.

I also made headway as my friend, George, lifted my spirits every time he visited me. Like my easel, he built a wheelchair lap tray—like a TV tray—that sat on my chair a few inches above my knees in the spring of '94. It was interesting that I felt better, less exposed, with the tray in place. Strangely, I had more confidence being around people as I hid behind it—less bothered by the stares. It also served other purposes. My family and caregivers gave me food and drinks that sat on it—making eating easier. And Jacob and his belongings sat on it, too.

Adding to the growing list of positives in our life, we occasionally borrowed an accessible van to venture out and watch a boxing match or drive to my parents. I felt less incarcerated with the freedom it represented. The need to get out whenever we wanted inspired us to look for a van of our own. And shortly after the search began, an opportunity presented itself. By spring, we had an accessible means of transportation. It was a piece of the puzzle I didn't realize I needed. The freedom it gave me by simply knowing it was there, outside in the parking lot, made me feel more complete.

With a growing positivity, I looked forward to escaping the apartment. Leaving the confines of the facility—an environment that seniors migrate to because their bodies or mental faculties begin failing them—was an act of defiance for me. I didn't belong there. Simply sitting in the van was therapy. So, we tried to visit several places and make every outing as fun, productive, and LONG as possible. We quickly became comfortable using the ramp, door switches, and wheelchair lock. And we often made plans to pick up food for lunch and go to the park—therapy.

Ebb and Flow

One afternoon, Sylvia was driving us along our usual route through town. She wasn't focused on the location or the grocery list—just driving, like any other day. As we approached an intersection, she didn't notice the four-door sedan speeding toward us. The driver of that car was distracted by her children in the back seat and failed to notice the stop sign looming ahead.

In an instant, the sunny afternoon turned dark. There was no warning—no blaring horn, no screech of tires. Just silence, until it happened. Out of the corner of my eye, I caught a flash of color a split second before my head slammed into the side window. The impact was so intense that our van spun 180 degrees, skidding across the intersection for 30 feet. In a matter of seconds, our lives took two steps back.

When the chaos settled, I found myself slumped in my chair, head down, possibly with broken bones. I felt beaten, but I was conscious. Jacob, confused but unharmed, broke the silence, asking if we'd been in a crash—his calm voice a strange source of reassurance. Sylvia and my caregiver were shaken, bruised, and in pain, but thankfully, nothing seemed too serious.

The crash had been traumatic, but considering the severity of the impact, we were lucky. Still, my first emotions were anger and frustration. Sylvia, too, was livid, shouting, "*How could this happen again?*"

As we tried to assess each other's injuries, the driver who hit us approached the van, her face full of concern. She wasn't hurt. Sylvia was ready to vent her anger, but fortunately, a nearby policeman stepped in before she could grab the woman—a mother of two—realizing just how close we had all come to something much worse.

A few minutes later, Dennis Calsen from the daycare arrived with the fire department. He quickly scooped Jacob up and invited him to sit in the fire truck—a dream for most kids—helping to ease his confusion and anxiety. Meanwhile, the firemen worked to extract me from the van and untangle my twisted chair. Paramedics evaluated all of us on the way to the hospital.

Sylvia and my caregiver were discharged within a couple of hours, shaken but okay, despite the significant bruising. I had a broken arm, but it wasn't displaced, and aside from that, I was released with little more than bruises.

Our van was destroyed, and my wheelchair bent beyond repair. The physical damage was clear, but our emotional wounds were even more raw. The progress we had made felt undone, taking two steps back in an instant. For our faith and my spirit, this was a test—a moment that demanded resilience.

The crash gave me yet another reason to scream silently inside, but I had to manage my anger. Over the next few weeks, as we began to recover, life resumed its rhythm. Sylvia returned to work, Jacob went back to daycare, and my caregiver found a new job. Meanwhile, I was left grappling with the lingering question: why did this happen? I searched for some meaning behind yet another stroke of bad luck. But there were no answers.

Insurance paid for a van rental after a couple of weeks. But without a usable wheelchair, I couldn't take advantage of it. Adding insult to injury, I was confined to my bed for 67 days until they could order another chair and deliver it. It was all very frustrating and overwhelming—the weeks trapped in a mattress prison AGAIN. I had to work hard at not being sad. Despondency after the crash would have been a fitting response. However, I searched for the silver lining in our misfortune—part of the stubborn nature nurtured by my father.

The loss of transportation was certainly hardest for Sylvia because she didn't want me to feel worse than I already did. When someone you care about struggles, it's worse than when you struggle. Her doubts were reinforced after the gut punch. I tried to make the best of an already crappy situation—not just for me, for her too. Learning to draw while stuck in bed helped mitigate the impact of the wreck. That's all it did.

We reached out to an attorney friend to help us deal with insurance issues from the accident. His involvement eased the strain we initially felt as he helped expedite repairs to our van and replace my chair. Then, in spring, he informed us we received a small settlement worth a few thousand dollars. It wasn't much. But we had just enough to pay closing costs for a small home. The most important outcome from this incident was that we were learning to dust ourselves off and get back up. Could we continue getting knocked down? What happened wasn't fair. However, I was tired of feeling broken. And Sylvia and Jacob needed me.

After our van was repaired and returned, I eventually received my wheelchair. With the two pieces in place, getting out again felt more liberating than the first time I left the apartment. I was cautious and anxious when I rode following the crash—reflexively slamming my feet on the brakes every time we came to a stop to prevent a repeat. And I became a terrible backseat driver. But because I didn't feel confined—trapped at home—I could inhale and look forward to the future.

Sitting in my wheelchair again, finding a rhythm, we drove to see people and places in the community while watching fall turn to winter. The ability to participate gave me an idealistic view about fitting in, about myself. I felt more normal as I stayed in touch with the world beyond the retirement home. I felt like I had left town for a while and returned to an unfamiliar city—like when you move away and come back to new roads and buildings you've never noticed before.

Eager to be a part of life, we grew less wary. Challenges were always around the corner—my disability a never-ending influence. However, we faced obstacles that many encountered and figured out how to overcome.

An evolving perspective made the cumulative challenges feel like they were part of regular life.

With the help of others and our newly strengthened optimism, things were starting to look up.

Chapter 7

Learning to Play and Embrace Life

Each day was better than the last when we moved into our small brick home in the spring of 1995. Adapting to amended roles as spouse, parent, and son helped us settle into familiar responsibilities. Me—the sports-minded loving dad; Sylvia—the put-a-band-aid-on-it-to-make-it-feel-better mom; and Jacob—a kid who thought about play and food. I replaced harbored angst with hope as the sun's warmth on my face and the subtle changes I could see in my family were enough reason to feel grateful. The significance of this place buoyed us because we chose to be there. Unlike the senior retirement facility that became home because it provided accessibility and made medical sense, we were there because Sylvia thought it was cute. Communication, a growing part of the new us, taught, reminded, and kept Sylvia and me present with each other's needs and emotions.

Progress came from a shared, determined love that was ever-present. Of course, there were bumps in the road. And we made mistakes. However, we didn't want to give up on each other—even through our unique struggles. That led to a growing, special relationship between Sylvia and me. We had to communicate to figure things out—a process threatened years before. As a result, we often ended our evenings with long conversations about hopes, dreams, and possibilities for the future.

Sylvia continued in her role as a loving and devoted mother with unwavering dedication. Her task was simple yet profound: after the accident, she had to shoulder a larger-than-usual share of the parenting duties as I adapted to my new reality of being disabled. Yet she embraced the challenge wholeheartedly.

For the sake of our son, she often tested her own boundaries. She patiently sat through video games. She stepped outside to shoot baskets on the hoop her brother Ramiro had bought for Jacob. She even engaged in playful roughhousing with Jacob, their shared laughter nourishing my soul.

I was thankful for her persistence and the joy she brought to Jacob. Yet, beneath my gratitude, there was a sting of sorrow. I hated my inability to help her like a typical dad, to share in those moments of play and support. Despite this, Sylvia's love and strength shone through, resilient and devoted to our family.

I didn't feel as defeated as I had during the first three years of my life as a quadriplegic. However, Jacob and I had to find new ways to interact because of my limitations, which was a sensitive issue. When he was born, the doctor asked if I wanted to cut his umbilical cord. As I held the scissors, I imagined playing catch with him at a ballpark years into the future and running behind him as he balanced on his first bicycle without training wheels. The pieces of my heart continued to crumble, knowing these things would never happen.

Determined to connect with my son in any way I could, I tried to be creative. One day, as he played with his plastic X-Men figures strewn all over the couch, I asked him which characters were the bad guys and which were the good ones. He was excited by my interest and eagerly described each hero and villain. His enthusiasm grew even more when I told him I wanted to play, too.

The wheels began to turn, and I came up with an idea. "Jacob, let's put all your X-Men on my lap-tray," I explained. After he gathered them, I asked him to find the pointer mouth stick I used to turn the pages of a book and type on a keyboard. This time, though, it was for something else. Once he placed it in my mouth, I mumbled, "Okay, Jacob, I'm going to flick your X-men—with my mouth—off the lap tray. If they land on their backs, they're still alive. If they land on their faces, they didn't make it."

As the plastic figures flew across the floor, Jacob couldn't help but giggle while I narrated an incredible and tense battle, ejecting the combatants one at a time. It was silly yet cathartic in the best of ways, as we learned and laughed together.

Playing with Jacob again made me feel how a father feels when his son first reaches up to hold his hand—that overwhelming sense that I would do anything for him.

In addition to the battles waged in our home, Jacob and my nephews enjoyed playing video games, golfing, and a game everyone calls lava. My heart healed as I cheered for their games, taught them golf, and helped set up the lava course. I was finding ways to participate—to be a dad.

The gradual accumulation of good, wholesome experiences helped my emotional healing. I began lowering my defenses, hoping for the next happy thing coming around the bend. But false expectations are detrimental, so I tried to remain realistic, even as hope grew each time I accomplished a task that seemed impossible. Beyond the psychological back-and-forth that hindered steady progress, physical obstacles built into a disabled life will always be reminders that I will never be the same.

Some challenges are less obvious, like bumpy lawns or leaning sidewalks for a wheelchair user. Other disability inconveniences are brutal. For instance, in our apartment, I could not shower at home because the bathroom was inaccessible. So I received a bed bath every morning. These baths were acceptable, even pleasant. But I missed the feeling of water spraying on my face and body. Showers are cleansing in ways beyond washing off sweat and dead skin cells. Feeling clean is also psychological, helping you experience a sense of order. The enveloping warmth of a shower on a cold morning is a great way to start your day. But I could not experience that where we were.

Taking stock and counting my blessings, I realized I had taken so much for granted—even a simple shower.

There was a subtle internal battle taking place within me. Not only was I cautious, but I also expected failure—a longtime insecurity. The struggle to understand why the accident happened, colored by feelings of inadequacy, kept me off balance. Sometimes, I felt like my disability made finding the upside to my life impossible as I looked for the silver lining in difficult situations—even as people rescued us along our journey. Terri, who helped save my life the night of my accident, was one such person.

In the spring of 1995, Terri surprised Jacob with a chocolate Labrador puppy. We hadn't seen her since my accident. And she wanted to see how I was doing. The gift was a way to break the ice and achieve that. For us, adding a puppy to our family felt like a "normal" thing to do—something that families do out of love for their children. It represented an ideal I imagined when I first met Sylvia: the white picket fence and a dog. Nina, the puppy, was a piece of that storybook ending.

When she came to our home, I was honored to thank Terri for helping save my life and to hear how she ended up in the right place at the right time. Although she was tied to the awful events of November 9th, her visit wasn't marked by sadness. Instead, she gently steered us in the right direction. Still, I found myself processing every situation as either normal or abnormal, feeling as though my disability set me apart. Success, when it came, was something I welcomed—but always with a bit of hesitation.

The internal battle continued. On one hand, I cherished moments of joy and connection, like Terri's visit and welcoming Nina into our family. On the other hand, I wrestled with feelings of inadequacy and the weight of my limitations. This constant tension made it difficult to fully embrace the positive aspects of life. But I kept moving forward, drawing strength from the love and support of those around me.

Kindness and encouragement from our family and friends were always there. Their love was unwavering. But at times, I felt more of their sympathy than their empathy. I couldn't help but focus on the negatives—especially in moments that called for typical father-son or husband-wife activities. Still, as we moved forward, my outlook slowly began to shift. It was almost imperceptible because, even in the most uplifting moments, I remained guarded. But somewhere along the way, the change happened.

The scale began to tip. I can't do most things like everyone else, but I can still do them—with help.

As I wrestled with these two voices, my perspective started to change. The question wasn't whether life would ever become easy; it was whether I was happy with *this* life. With the unwavering support of family and friends, especially Sylvia and Jacob, my thoughts turned less to mortality and more to the future. Strength, comfort, and creativity began to help me see myself as more capable, finding new ways to be there for them—and for myself.

Time

A friend once told me I have more time than most to consider my choices. He meant it as a compliment. Hopefully, I make the right decision while overthinking when approaching a dilemma. But I often do so obsessively and compulsively because I have a lot of surplus time—time people reserve for able-bodied endeavors. So, my friend is correct in his assessment. I overthink, worrying about things I can't control.

Most people have a lot on their plates that demands their full attention. Success in each endeavor requires dedicated time. Work requires adequate time to earn enough money to pay for transportation, a place to live, and food to eat. It takes time to exercise, pursue interests like the arts, and connect and socialize with those you love and care about, especially your kids. Some aspects of our lives do not get enough attention for us to become good at. There is only so much time. And most don't have enough.

Excess time for me was an unexpected parenting perk my disability afforded me. When Jacob walked in the front door from school each day, his response was, "Dad, I'm home." He knew I was there for him EVERY day because of my disability—because I'm unable to exercise or work a nine-to-five job. My attention was for him.

But no one has *the* parenting playbook. All parents have doubts—it was the same for me. Parenting is not easy. I frequently question my parenting ability because I am disabled. However, after weighing the positives of having plenty of time for Jacob and Sylvia, I felt better about being a disabled parent.

I also valued my time alone just as much as spending time with my family. It was difficult for me to feel independent because I need assistance with almost everything. If I'm hungry, want to go somewhere, or I'm cold and need a blanket, someone has to help me. Dependence generates a lack of self-confidence. But at Rancho, an Environmental Control Unit (ECU) was provided by rehab staff. This allowed me to answer the phone and operate my TV and bed. It also helped me feel independent because I could be alone—with a degree of control.

Through the first years after my accident, I therapeutically allowed the emotion I kept concealed to come forth when I was by myself—usually by yelling as loudly as I could. I can't scream very loudly because I can't neurogenically use my muscles to push air from my lungs. But the cleansing release of emotion without the worry that I might hurt others allowed me to move closer toward the place where acceptance opened the door to a future I couldn't imagine yet. I loved being alone because I felt more normal.

We had settled into various routines at home, both during the day and in the evening. The consistency was reassuring. Evenings were particularly ideal for me to be alone.

One crisp fall evening, Sylvia and Jacob popped into my room to say they were heading to the grocery store—a routine they both loved. They wouldn't be gone long, just picking up a few essentials. For Jacob, strolling the aisles with his mom was a small adventure, always on the lookout for his favorite snacks. It had become their special time to connect, an effortless but cherished way to bond.

While Sylvia and Jacob were out, I used my Ezra (ECU) to flip through television channels or answer the phone, savoring my independence. Their outings were positive for everyone. Shortly after they left, our kitten, Shadow, jumped up on Sylvia's twin bed next to mine for a nap, providing me with some company.

Before I continue, I need to explain something about quadriplegia. Spasticity is very common in quads. It can present as muscle stiffness, uncontrollable muscle twitching, or an overall body spasm. For me, my fingers, toes, or even my legs sometimes twitch without warning. It's usually no big deal.

I was happy with each chance to feel independent. So, when Jacob and Sylvia left, I found a sports event I liked and tilted my bed back to relax. As I watched basketball, I noticed my left big toe steadily twitching. I generally use spasticity to gauge my health. Whenever I experience atypical clamminess or twitching/spasms, I know there is something wrong with my body—dysreflexia. But spasms in bed are usually benign. What was different about the situation this time was that the twitching had woken the primal, innate instinct of our not-*yet*-asleep kitten. It wasn't long before the predatory stalk of a carnivore inched closer and closer to my foot. Even though the normal progression of a stalking carnivore made it inevitable, I was surprised by Shadow's new lack of a cuddly persona. Still, it was a bit amusing when he finally POUNCED! I wasn't too concerned. But I was curious what would happen next. Little did I know.

The attack of the beast was like watching an episode of a wild *Animal Planet* TV show—only with a tiny, stuffed animal-looking kitten, devoid of any cuddliness. As he continued his assault, moving to latch onto my foot and give my toe a "lethal neck wound," my entire leg began to bounce as his tiny, needle-like claws dug into my flesh. I was glad I couldn't feel what would have been painful cat wounds. Sadly, the bouncing only encouraged him to strengthen his grip on my foot, causing even more vigorous convulsions.

Then, unbelievably, the attack escalated, and I became a bit concerned about his intent. I started wondering if he seriously wanted to eat my toe! More rattled now, I started yelling at my unlikely foe, to no avail, as my body responded violently to the aggression. The exchange was surreal, seeing him gnaw on my toe like a fresh, not-yet-dead kill—he the predator, and me the prey. I couldn't believe it. As the assault continued, I yelled as loud as I could, hoping to dissuade him. But he just lifted his head high enough to look at me and release a deep, guttural, evil little growl. It quickly became apparent he wasn't willing to share his prize with anyone.

At times during the carnage, I even thought about spitting at him. However, I knew I would probably spit on myself and leave evidence of the disturbed individual I'd become. It wouldn't have worked anyway. So, for 20 minutes, I tried to ignore the massacre unfolding before me. Able to do little but watch television as my body reacted to what my nemesis was doing, I forcibly learned patience.

After what seemed like forever, he suddenly grew tired and left my bloody foot and toe corpses. Then he casually walked over my right leg onto Sylvia's bed, curled up into a ball, and fell asleep.

I was defeated when Sylvia and Jacob returned home. Sylvia immediately noticed millions of dots of blood covering my foot and toe—after she gave me the requisite kiss.

"Oh my gosh! What happened?" she exclaimed, a shocked look on her face. My toe had suffered the brunt of Shadow's aggression, looking like he had used it as a pin cushion. And Sylvia could see I was wrestling with my sanity when I responded. "It was that little shit!" As I stared at my antagonist, he reminded me I had a way to go to control my emotions—having let this three-pound fluff ball bring forth feelings I didn't think I had in me.

Not many days after the mugging, as I contemplated his future, Shadow chewed through the wires of my wheelchair—disabling it. That was the last straw! Our response? Shadow was gifted to my parents to terrorize them for a while. And Jacob got a hamster named Shaq.

Every double-edged experience taught us a valuable lesson for the future. While Sylvia focused on Jacob, putting him first in everything, she continued to hurt because she saw me in pain. She often expressed anger and doubts about faith as I tried to reassure her that we would find our way—even if I didn't have all the answers. We were conflicted. But we leaned on our collective strength.

I started believing I could be a successful father and a supportive husband because the difficulties we encountered pushed me to find solutions. We also grew closer emotionally and in tune with each other as we depended on each other. For a time, Sylvia handled the load and kept our family together. Now, I wanted them to lean on me. I wanted her to worry less.

Searching for creative ways to stay active and relevant, I coached Jacob by explaining how to stand, swing a bat, and shoot a ball. I had to be very descriptive because of his age and my limitations. I didn't want Sylvia to stress about this—about Jacob needing someone to teach him sports—if I could do my part. All I had was my voice and a singular approach to being a good dad and spouse. Surprisingly, my efforts to "stay in the game" created unexpected by-products of our unique relationship. Jacob learned to listen more intently than most children need to, creating a uniquely strong bond between us. And he also worried less.

Staying in step, Sylvia became a Chicago Bulls fan even though she knew little about the sport. And Sylvia also bought Jacob Fleer, Topps, and Upper Deck trading cards that made his day. She attempted almost everything.

We entered our third spring at the brick house, and with spring came the start of sports season. Like many parents, I had once imagined my child playing sports, picturing baseball as part of the classic American summer experience. Years earlier, I dreamed of sharing that father-son bond with Jacob on the field. But after my accident, everything changed. So, Sylvia stepped in and took him to his first T-ball practice. And for the next two years, we cheered from the sidelines as he ran the bases, half-confused—just like most of the kids his age.

In April of that year, Sylvia signed Jacob up for coach-pitch baseball, the next step up from T-ball. This season would be different—

someone would actually be pitching to him. That posed a challenge. Sylvia would sometimes toss him wiffle balls, but her flinchy throws made for more laughs than practice. Still, her efforts to do anything for Jacob were wind in my sails. Deep down, I longed to step in and fulfill a dream of my own. Then, during one of those pitching sessions, a distant memory surfaced, offering me a glimmer of hope.

I remembered something I saw at a softball tournament I participated in several years before my accident. As I played catch between softball fields preparing for a game, I witnessed a little boy pitching wiffle balls to himself with a machine. The contraption had a spinning plastic wheel and a small tube-like hopper containing a few wiffle balls. Connected to it was a 15-foot tube with a small bulb—like that on a blood pressure cuff.

As I watched, he retrieved the plastic balls he'd already hit, returned, and placed them in the machine, then the future all-star walked a small distance from the toy, stepped on the bulb, and a pneumatic mechanism released a ball onto a spinning wheel—ejecting it as he swung the bat like a pro.

The device was so clever and memorable because he was pitching to himself! He was alone, independent of an adult. I was sure that memory could help our situation. The more I thought about it, the more I felt the toy represented success as a parent. If it worked, it would be a solution *I* found—not giving up because of an obstacle.

After calling incessantly for a week, I finally found someone who knew of the toy I described. I ordered the machine from Toys 'R' Us and waited like a kid for Christmas. When it arrived, we couldn't put it together fast enough.

We set up the pitching machine in our backyard following a few adjustments. Eager to try it out, I was nervous as I wheeled next to it. I planned to sit across from him as I triggered the machine—with my mouth. Once I was in place, I excitedly asked Jacob to get ready about 12 feet away. The first time I blew into the tube and watched the first pitch fly towards Jacob, I was overwhelmed in a good way—I had created the same effect as the average father pitching to his son. After adjusting how far the ball flew, Jacob set up to swing away. Then, when he lined one past me the first time, Sylvia, Jacob, and I laughed. And I fought hard to keep from crying. As each consecutive pitch flew toward my son, I became more emotional.

The unlikely piece of equipment worked better than I imagined and lessened the weight I felt when I thought about being in a wheelchair—about not being able to play catch with my son. Over the next few weeks, Jacob pelted me in the face and body—too many times to count. And I healed with each ball that found its unintended target.

During years of progress, another topic emerged from the late-night conversations Sylvia and I often had. We began discussing our desire to have more kids. It was a challenging discussion due to the improbability of a quadriplegic having children. Still, the subject began to color the pages of dreams for an alternate future—a future that never happened.

Sylvia, who had many siblings and valued the blessings of a large family, began sharing her dreams of a little girl. But the improbability of conceiving became a new source of sadness related to the accident. I felt guilty when she mentioned how cute baby girls' clothes looked and imagined the bond between mother and daughter. Her heartache was my fault. Sometimes she cried while talking out loud—with no malice or blame in her voice. I didn't want her to hurt and was afraid to talk about it due to the emotions involved. However, during these moments, we were as close as ever, leaning on each other through the heartache.

The communication between Sylvia and I continued improving, even as we faced difficult challenges. During our conversations, we also discussed solutions to other obstacles, goals, and dreams we shared. We weren't ready for big changes yet, but I began to hope.

We had found a groove with help from family, friends, and each other as the mood during our years at the brick house consistently trended up. Stability replaced the chaos that had affected Jacob over the last few years. His constants were school, making friends, playing sports, and adapting as Sylvia and I reassured him we were fine. It was also important to me for Sylvia to take a break from disability—from words like wheelchair, paralyzed, and Hoyer. She was also doing better. But everyone needs a break now and then. Our consolation was that her work environment provided routine and an outlet for Sylvia while distracting her from worrying about me—her friends were a constant support.

I discovered a sense of purpose in providing support for our family in any way I could. The satisfaction I derived from this role bolstered my spirits, a role thought to be impossible for a long time. With each instance where my efforts made a difference for them, I found myself growing more self-assured. Concerned about my emotional state, Sylvia would often inquire, "Are you okay?" My response, "I'm okay, Mama," seemed to alleviate some of her worries, and as a result, mine dissipated as well. The truth is, I've been enduring constant pain since my accident. Nevertheless, I feel it's my responsibility to offer them reassurance and to maintain a smiling facade, despite the pain, so they won't worry. I am determined to protect them.

Receiving hope, and boosts to our morale, continued at every stage of our new life. When we first settled into our home, I was pleasantly surprised to discover that a childhood friend, whom I hadn't crossed paths with since my accident, was living just 50 yards away, across the street. Our friendship had been rooted in our shared love for sports and mutual connections—friends from neighboring schools.

But seeing him, the worrisome thing—the self-conscious thing—was that Mando remembered me as an active, able-bodied friend, not someone in a wheelchair. This made me apprehensive about how he would react to my disability and the noticeable changes in my body since the accident. When I encountered many of my old friends for the first time after my accident, I couldn't shake off the anxiety about what they might be thinking. I felt incredibly vulnerable. However, when Mando, along with George and my two friends, came to visit, my worries dissipated. He was naturally at ease as he assisted me with meals or drinks during the first reacquainting couple of months—showing a remarkable disposition for caregiving. His efforts in teaching Jacob about sports cards were truly meaningful. And Mando's kindness extended to Sylvia, offering support during the highs and lows of those initial years. In various ways, Mando stepped in to help us when we needed it the most.

Adding to my wishful connection with the outside world, I formed an unexpected friendship with George. One of the most tangible ways he supported me was through his craftsmanship, building adaptive equipment tailored to my needs. But our conversations went far beyond disability. We often spoke about participation and gratitude, and each encounter subtly shifted my perspective. Our relationship began to feel more personal, a bridge between my world and the able-bodied. George wasn't just the occupational therapist who assisted me; in my mind, he was becoming my friend.

Beyond creating equipment for me, George built adaptive tools for others—like an accessible table or a makeup carousel for a newly disabled parent trying to stay connected to life. His skills weren't limited to function; he also crafted beautiful wooden shadow boxes and other artistic pieces, which he sold at arts and crafts fairs.

Throughout my recovery, George became one of my biggest cheerleaders, offering steady encouragement. His belief in me gave me the confidence to try new things—like learning to draw with my mouth and embracing life as a disabled person. In time, I found myself joining him at those arts and crafts fairs, displaying the charcoal drawings I had begun to create.

We found ourselves out and about, among people who were genuinely interested in my art and our family's story. And I made significant psychological strides, becoming less concerned about the stares. Each accomplishment was like therapy, and every event Sylvia and I attended was worth far more than the few dollars we made. It was all part of the healing process—a direct result of George's influence.

Our family was accomplishing many of the things I imagined impossible after the accident. We were present with each other—stepping lightly as we walked about rough ground. And we were even finding solutions to many of the problems that arose. The discussions of hopes and dreams helped us make sense of everything we lost. But we didn't imagine the conversations would lead to anything real. Speaking out loud, we were just trying to get by—to continue managing.

Focusing on Sylvia and Jacob, speaking with friends, and learning art helped me feel alive. But there were still unanswered questions about the most unfair aspects of my new life. I questioned the likelihood of ever being a father again. On a lesser level of want, I also longed for an accessible bathroom. And there were plenty of other issues in our lives that needed attention. So, we weren't ready for any life-changing decisions yet. But the most unexpected whisper during those late nights was, "Maybe we can have a little girl." We had come so far. Just thinking about it made us feel good.

Hope painted the next chapter of our lives.

Chapter 8

The Last Months at Home

Sylvia and I continued growing closer, inspired by our evening discussions and epiphanies. Sylvia worked hard to make our small brick house a home. She made interior cosmetic changes, exposing a vinyl kitchen floor to reveal hardwood and replacing old curtains with vertical blinds in our living room. Outside, she worked in the yard planting bushes and flowers. She was determined to improve and fix anything that needed fixing.

I kept busy trying to solve puzzles consistent with a quadriplegic life, like finding someone to install a door in our bedroom to access our bumpy backyard. Jacob also found his groove with his dog in tow—playing in the backyard on irrigation day.

We all made steady progress during those first years—physically, emotionally, and psychologically. Discussing an accessible home and having a baby were approachable subjects now as confidence grew in us. And I began acknowledging—even scrutinizing—the accident without debilitating heartache.

The permanence of my broken body and its limitations still burned—though less fiercely now.

Yes, I will always have moments of internal frustration; I am a quadriplegic, after all! But who doesn't question life's tests? It took several years to come to terms with living in a disabled body. Yet, as I began to look toward the future, the angst about "being normal" receded.

My perspective shifted: there isn't a specific normal.

I have fears, dreams, wants, and desires like everyone else. Despite the differences, I still have my needs met. My thirst, hunger, passions, and desires *are* satisfied. This gradual shift in my sense of self—the psychology of self—allowed me to re-engage with life.

My frail body is a constant reminder of my physical weakness. I fought back tears the first time I saw myself in a full-length mirror—my atrophied body and new station in life staring back at me. Yet the purpose I found through volunteering, something I once thought out of reach, replaced my doubt, fear, and worry. Over time, I focused less on my weaknesses and more on how I could help others.

Immediately after the accident, I was too close to the trees to see the forest. I couldn't see that my health and perspective were steadily improving. The reality of how different my life was from the life I used to know—and the life I still wished for—impeded my progress. But slowly, as our family's outlook evolved, those subtle, incremental gains at home began to improve our lives.

Visiting the Elks Rehabilitation Center to speak with patients further boosted my self-esteem. After the accident, my family and friends responded to my wheelchair and disability with worry, condolence, and empathy. At the hospital, though, staff and patients reacted to my presence with appreciation and gratitude—understanding that the questions, struggles, and emotions they faced might be like mine.

My appreciation for altruism—for doing something that wasn't about me, something bigger than myself—became a catalyst for my healing. For most people, living a purposeful life is fundamental to mental well-being. Even the simplest responsibilities—caring for flowers at a local park or preparing an elderly neighbor's lunch—can provide a reason to wake up every morning. Volunteering at the hospital became one of my reasons. I couldn't always tell how much of an impact I had, but it was affirming to help others at Elks *because* of my disability—because being broken gave me a unique insight.

At times along this journey, I've noticed that people will glance at me and sometimes stare, certainly not being rude, but just wondering about my injury or feeling bad about my situation. I think the perception is that because you're in a wheelchair, you're supposed to be sad or depressed.

But the more I participated—helping my wife, teaching Jacob, volunteering—the more I felt like a husband, a dad, and a contributing member of society.

The visits to Elks were a big part of many of the epiphanies that helped assess my life. At one time, my younger self hoped to make a difference someday. And taking in every attitude-adjusting encounter I had at the hospital told me I was relevant. Nurtured by George, the patients, and the staff, I grew to dismiss my insecurities. I looked forward to getting out because of the influence the hospital had on me. The confidence it provided nurtured my progress as a person.

The evolving story of overcoming continued at home, lifted by the positive influences that happened in a world that still felt foreign.

And an awareness of how different my life was made the successes seem huge. However, it also made the failures seem even bigger. Finding access via a loading dock to a previously inaccessible building was pretty cool. Not being able to attend a friend's wedding reception because of inaccessibility stinks. But we were becoming more resilient each day.

Highs and Lows at Home

Autumn and the holiday season came and went during our last months at the brick house. After the new year, an incident brought together my love of sports, family, and some of the baby steps we were taking. The Broncos and Falcons were set to face off in the Super Bowl—a highlight of the sports calendar and a connection to my past. I'd always loved playing football in high school and with family at Thanksgiving, and I enjoyed picking teams for football pools. The Super Bowl wasn't just another game; it was a reminder of good times, even if those memories now carried a bittersweet sadness.

This Super Bowl party at my parents' house wasn't just about sports or reminiscing about the old days. Not anymore. In the past, I only worried about pacing myself with food and drinks—milling about and sampling wings, chips, and beer. Accessibility was never a concern. But now, the reality was different. I had to think about how accessible the space was, and after working through the self-consciousness of asking awkward, revealing questions, I was actually looking forward to leaving the house.

The get-together ticked many boxes on the list of "Things That Can Help a Quad Feel Good." A Super Bowl party brings people together—family, friends, and fun. It was a chance to decompress. While I couldn't roam from person to person or feed myself, I could still eat, laugh, and enjoy the experience. The evolving version of me was eager to see family and friends, share old memories, and create new ones.

We worked hard, overcoming each challenge as it arose. Acquiring an old accessible van was another piece of the puzzle, allowing me to be part of the "regular" world again. I was eager to load up and go anywhere—Elks, the golf course, dinner. So, traveling to the Super Bowl party should have been no big deal.

Unsurprisingly, Super Bowl Sunday arrived in a frenzy. We had planned for the day, yet for me, it felt like a surprise. Since the accident, I almost expected fun, planned events to fail or not happen at all. That morning, Sylvia helped get me ready before preparing herself. Fortunately, Jacob had spent the night with his cousins, so there was no need to rush him along—less stress for us. I was eager to leave the house and be with family. Events like this felt ordinary, something I craved. As I imagined the food and my brother's wisecracks, Sylvia gathered everything we needed, including the food we were bringing. She loaded our Dodge Caravan, then returned to help me into the cold February afternoon, locking the front door behind us.

I followed her out, my anticipation growing as Sylvia lowered the accessible ramp onto the yard so I could wheel in, ready for the ambiance and fun that only a family party can bring. Nudging the joystick of my wheelchair with my chin, I moved forward while Sylvia climbed into the van and waited for me.

Our front yard was about a foot higher than the street because previous owners had built an aesthetic gradual slope on the front of the yard to meet the lower curb—about six feet. As such, the accessible ramp sat level like a bridge because it sat on higher ground—usually angled down when in a parking lot.

I wheeled to where the slope began and proceeded down the slight gradient to enter the van. As I leveled onto the ramp, I released my joystick to pause the descent and check my alignment. I had done this hundreds of times before. But this time, the wheelchair's electronics malfunctioned. Instead of stopping, the chair kept rolling to the right, misaligning the front wheel and setting off a terrible chain of events.

I felt my body lurch as the chair tipped, and I immediately knew I was in trouble. Sylvia's terrified expression from the driver's seat only heightened the dread as the slow-motion collapse continued. Powerless to stop it, I instinctively tried to reach out—an impossible attempt to halt the inevitable. But all I could do was brace myself mentally for the impact as the surreal moment unfolded.

I turned my head, hoping to limit the damage as my face collided with the curb. The fall was so violent that I blacked out.

Sylvia panicked when I came to, as she futilely tried to lift my chair. But the weight of me and the chair was considerable. She understood my vulnerability and worried I had sustained a life-threatening head injury or, at the very least, broken bones. She was also frantic because, without anyone else around, I was NOT getting off the frozen ground without assistance. So, there I lay, stunned and in pain. I remembered that a mother and her two daughters recently moved next door. Unfortunately, there seemed to be no activity there—possibly out to a party somewhere. Sylvia ran over anyway, and we got lucky. When Sylvia described the situation to the woman who answered the door and asked her to help, she and her two teenage daughters quickly ran over.

They were shocked to find me and my wheelchair sprawled on the ground. We hadn't met them yet, and they didn't know anything about us. In another situation, I would've preferred their introduction to quadriplegia to come through one of my spasms during a casual conversation in the driveway. Instead, they hesitantly rushed over to lift me from the gutter as Sylvia calmly instructed them on how to help.

Meeting new people after my injury often felt clumsy—even in the best of circumstances. As Sylvia and I thanked them once they got me back on four wheels, it wasn't exactly how we wanted to say, *"Nice to meet you, neighbor. We're Sylvia and Non."* From their perspective, it must have been a bizarre and awkward encounter. Unsurprisingly, we never spoke to them after that—the strange moment our only interaction.

Still dazed, I felt—and probably looked—like I'd just taken a jab from Mike Tyson. Instinctively, Sylvia wanted to rush me to the hospital, suggesting I should get x-rays of my face. But I didn't want her to worry or ruin the day over a bump on the head. Her worry had become one of my main concerns, as it seemed she'd spent more time being anxious than not over the years. The day's mood would depend on how I responded to the discomfort and how I helped my wife through it.

So, I reassured her: *"I'm fine, Mama."* Ever since we returned from rehab in California, it felt like my emotions were contagious. If I was quiet, the room followed suit. When I laughed, it was like my friends and family breathed a collective sigh of relief. Today was no different. If I could help it, Sylvia would put her worry aside, and the party would give everyone a chance to forget about my disability for a few hours. At least, that was my hope.

Thankfully, after some persuasion, Sylvia capitulated, and we skipped the ER trip. It turns out crossing your eyes instead of your fingers to anchor a wish can work. Still, concern weighed heavily on her, and she convinced me to at least lie down for a bit. Once she composed herself, she notified my parents of the event.

Sylvia found it challenging to keep them from worrying since they responded to anything related to my disability with excessive concern—typical parents. They understood how much I had been looking forward to this day. After Sylvia explained that I was okay, they proposed bringing the party to us, hoping to lift our spirits.

I had a swollen face and was sore, but I was determined to watch the game with my family. So, I begged a bit more, crossed my eyes for good measure, and finally, Sylvia agreed, helping me back into my chair before they arrived. After everything, we were going to enjoy the day.

The overwhelming sympathy they expressed when they arrived felt uncomfortably excessive. Yet their steadfast support and habitually playful nature lightened the mood. Throughout the afternoon, my family consoled me and shared laughs about the alarming incident. We enjoyed ourselves, eating and following the game. Halftime football pool winnings and news the following day of zero fractures hastened my recovery.

Days later, as I reflected on that crazy day, I realized the optimism about how life was improving outweighed any lingering doubts. Surprisingly, the fall had a minimal impact on my outlook. We even found some facetious humor in it, often joking about my hard head.

Sharing a smile with others feels good—especially with family. I frequently observed the magic a wink and a smile can create. Kindness and a warm facade allowed my family to see resilience in me, rather than just the struggle of coping with my disability. The fall reinforced the idea that I could help myself and others—simply by maintaining a good attitude.

Confidence was growing in me, in part because of George. As that confidence took root, my friend asked if I could visit with a patient he had spoken to about me. That's how I first began volunteering at the hospital. Volunteering gave me the chance to help people who were hurting and afraid, struggling with injury, tragedy, or sorrow.

Each visit with patients connected me to emotions that shifted how I assessed my own life. When life throws challenges at you, it can be difficult for others to truly understand what you're going through. But these patients *did*—they wrestled with emotions I recognized intimately. Work, relationships, and financial stress can weigh heavily on anyone, but health issues are uniquely personal, often leading to heartache and isolation.

Moreover, patients couldn't say, "*You don't understand how hard this is. You don't know what it's like!*" when I sat with them at their bedsides. This truth allowed me to simply *be* there without needing to break through their defenses. All I needed was a smile. Or even a nonplussed look was enough to grant me permission to stay. They knew that I hurt every second of every minute of every day. I could relate to their psychological and physical struggles in ways that required no words. Advice wasn't necessary—because that wasn't what they wanted or needed. What they sought, more than anything, was someone who could help them make sense of their burden. They wanted to see someone who still functioned after tragedy—or at least speak with someone who understood the emotional monologue running through their mind.

When the lost and broken eventually opened up, the questions they asked were the same ones we all wrestle with: "*Were you scared? Did you want to give up? Do you wish this hadn't happened?*"

What they needed from me was honesty. Even though these conversations exposed raw truths I wasn't always ready to face, I bargained with my emotions to be of help. Time and again, I saw how smiling—whether on the inside or out—affected the outcomes of these encounters.

I could help because, although doctors, therapists, and social workers are there to support patients, the interactions between patient and professional can sometimes be challenging and even ineffective. Hospital stays for life-changing afflictions force you to contend with fears, grief, and realities that I am uniquely aware of. This understanding created a bridge between the patients and me that professionals couldn't always establish.

When George first reached out to me, I was humbled to have the opportunity to participate. I was grateful that he thought of me, knowing I could fulfill a need. I learned that I still had a lot to give. Friendships with the occupational therapists, physical therapists, and other professionals at the hospital became a pleasant consequence of these visits. I soon realized that I volunteered for my friends as much as for the patients.

Volunteering, while altruistic, had a positive side effect: it was also indirectly self-serving. I received something in return.

Speaking with other patients created an exchange of sincerity that quietly replenished me, filling my glass with meaning and purpose.

The available time I had to spend at the hospital was another paradoxical benefit of my disability. When I volunteered at Elks and came home late—Jacob would question me and ask, "Where were you, Dad?" Being there all the time, as broken as I was, was comforting to Jacob. After explaining that I was at the hospital again, he would ask, "Is it your job, Dad? Do they give you money when you go?" His interest in my visits was less about a concern or understanding—it was maybe about making enough money to get him new X-Men. However, his questions created conversations. He was perplexed when I told him that it wasn't work. Jacob didn't yet understand altruism. "They need my help. So I go," I told him. It felt good to pass on something like this to my son. All because I was willing to share my pain with others.

A recently injured paraplegic patient George asked me to visit was especially memorable. Debbie was in her mid-30s and was doing outpatient therapy a couple of times a week.

With permission, George asked me to join him during patient therapies. Afterward, we visited over lunch to further get to know the patients. I found that lunchtime was an ideal way to provide a buffer between any awkward moments that might hamper an honest discussion between them and me. The buffer also helped to ensure the outcome of sharing my experience. It was like a first date. But instead of a possible romance, the goal was possible healing. To think I could swoop in, tell my story, and fix things was presumptuous. However, the responses encouraged me and helped me feel relevant.

George, Debbie, her daughter, my caregiver and I were there during our first meeting. In retrospect, I believe those moments—with every patient—should have been more uncomfortable than they were. Each conversation was unpredictable, given the circumstances. "Let's talk about your life-changing accident," was an awkward subject, yet the reason I was there. Surprisingly, the interactions were usually positive and filled with subtlety. Talking to Debbie and her daughter was like that—giving us confidence as we enjoyed our food. They appeared to be doing well. And the gift of a piece of my art Debbie previously admired in the hospital hallway seemed well received. I felt I received more than I gave during the visits with them. My hope for Debbie was for an easier road ahead. After visits like this end, you hope you have made a meaningful impact. But you usually never know.

Many years later, Sylvia and I participated in an art show nearby. I always looked forward to leaving the house and interacting with the outside world—especially at shows because they allow me to enjoy music and food with Sylvia while also creating income. Even though I never make much money, I feel I belong in life—connected to the community. Occasionally, we run into former patients when I'm out. And the encounters are often moving.

On the final day of this show, feeling drained by the bustling craft fair and the sweltering heat, I didn't recognize the young lady approaching our booth. She wore a comforting smile as she drew near and said, "You probably don't remember me. You went to the hospital and had lunch with my mom, Debbie, and me. I'm Layla." The flood of memories from our visits many years ago, combined with the presence of the young woman before me, warmed my heart. After introducing her to Sylvia and explaining the connection, I was eager to hear how her family was doing. So, I gently inquired, "How is your mom?" She paused for a moment, visibly struggling to contain her emotions. Then, with a quiver in her voice, she began recounting the time that had passed since our first meeting. "After rehab, my mom found a place where we could live. There were times when life was hard for our family. But my mom was always there for us and taught us to be tough."

The Debbie I'd met over lunch and physical therapy was a caring mother who didn't complain about her situation. As she adjusted to a disabled life, she was happy, smiling and laughing during our visits.

Layla continued, "You know the picture you gave us at the hospital? It sat above the couch. And sometimes, during times that were hard for us or when we complained, my mom pointed to the picture and would say, '*If he can do that . . .*'"

Hearing that my picture was a symbol of hope and determination was humbling. But the loss in Layla's story became more devastating: "A few years ago, my mom was in another terrible car accident and died. She had already been through so much. It wasn't fair. Then, we had to move quickly. And we were forced to leave most of our stuff behind, including the print.

"The picture you gave us meant so much to my mom—to all of us. But I didn't know how to reach you to replace it. And I thought I would never see you again. So I was really surprised to see you here."

As I emotionally processed the story of how Debbie had endured, the question that plagued me before raced through my mind again:

Why do some people suffer so much? My struggles have been formative—a hard place to advance from. But the loss of Layla's mom was simply unfair. Layla's resilience and bravery as she talked about her mom, however, showed how she was just like her—determined, head up. So her heart softened mine, and I was able to take away the best of Layla's spirit from the encounter. Meeting Layla as an adult—coming full circle—meant a lot.

We talked a bit more—all while fighting back tears. Then, as we sighed like you do after a good cry, Sylvia brought forward the lost print—one for her and one for her sister. Layla hugged us, grateful for the gesture. And we said goodbye.

It was an overwhelming, emotional moment. But Layla's and her mom's indelible will remind me—like so many others have along this journey—that it is possible to endure anything—and continue through the dark. Qualms with my perspective keep me on my toes, assessing and reassessing life's lessons. But Layla also addressed another question I often mull over—what happens after the visits with a patient end? Layla brought us a narrative that lessened the lingering self-doubt I felt.

Chapter 9

The Shower

The decision to finally pursue the dream of constructing an accessible home felt overwhelming. However, the evolution of our family was part of this next big step. I refused to settle for limited outcomes dictated by my deficits. Instead, I sought to embrace the next chapter in our journey and the possibilities ahead.

We had to educate ourselves about access to housing. Research led to an understanding of the infancy of what was known as the "accessibility movement" and motivated me as we learned about the Americans with Disabilities Act (ADA). Passed in 1990, two years before my accident, it created legislation that led to increasing access and opportunity for people with handicaps. For us this meant access in a home.

Accessible residential construction—including features such as wheelchair-accessible doors, low-threshold showers, and entryways—wasn't commonplace yet. However, we learned that some builders were aware of the various elements suggested by the ADA and were receptive. The information we gathered prompted us to reach out to a real estate friend and former teacher of mine who would know of available resources and the steps we needed to take. She'd heard about my accident. And she was eager to help, introducing us to a local construction company and a lender who could assist us.

The journey was eye-opening and emotionally invigorating, especially each time we checked off a task on our list. We felt immense joy as we searched for potential locations, learning along the way and dreaming out loud as we explored the town. Our hearts became invested in finding a new home, a place far removed from the weight of sadness.

Conversations with Hibbard Construction were rejuvenating. However, when we broached the subject of accessibility during an afternoon meeting, I surprised myself by my reaction. I couldn't access the yard, the kitchen, or Jacob's bedroom where we were, and the bathroom in our brick house wasn't set up for me either. We were addressing many issues simultaneously, many of which had negative connotations. I was okay with everything else but discussing the bathroom exposed feelings I chose to keep to myself.

The eventual transition from one house to another added to the trepidation, given the logistics of disability. Selling our current home before construction could begin was necessary because we worried about having two mortgages if the transition wasn't smooth. However, the possibility of finding an accessible rental if the new home wasn't ready in time heightened our fears.

After selling our home, one worry was resolved. However, securing a bank loan, coordinating builder schedules, making design choices, and finalizing the sale of our house forced us to search for a rental where we could stay for a few months during the construction of our new place. This became a significant problem.

We scoured the white pages for a while and were relieved to find someone understanding and flexible enough to offer us a short lease. But the rental we found had issues. It was small, with only one bedroom and two steps on the front stoop to traverse. And we nicknamed it "The Mouse House" due to its infestation of mice. For Jacob and me, the mice weren't so disturbing that we couldn't handle it. But Sylvia had to set mousetraps throughout the rental to rid us of the vermin.

I dodged mousetrap duty for obvious reasons. Jacob was curious like a typical kid and had no issue participating. He even found humor in every mousetrap snap that first week, which was a bit morbid. But Sylvia, uneasy, reluctantly showed Jacob how to set the traps and assigned him to mouse patrol—his curiosity an advantage. And she became thoroughly disgusted by the dead mice she dealt with during the three months we spent at The Mouse House.

Another stressor, the steps at the entry of The Mouse House were steep, making it frightening and dangerous for me to enter and exit. I had ramps that had been lent out and damaged years before and were now shorter, which made using them risky. We were fortunate to avert disaster for three months, navigating what felt like a circus ride every day.

Oh, and a colony of bees made a home inside our bathroom wall and there was nowhere for our pets to play!

Considering all the concessions we made while living there, it was a surprise that those summer days were so memorable and fun. One of the unexpected highlights happened each morning when Sylvia left for work, and I happily filled roles that gave me purpose and identity. I taught Jacob how to prepare box meals by adding meat and water to the contents and placing the dish in the oven. We also practiced golf in the shady neighborhood, as I lived vicariously through each of my son's swings.

At the time, Sylvia was studying to get certified in another imaging modality. Jacob and I were glad to help with her homework, reading her physics books and reviewing her exams with her. It was satisfying to be part of her work life, supporting her in small ways. Success in these small things and the growing closeness between Jacob, Sylvia, and me in our shared, odd environment distracted us from the inconveniences of mice, bees, and not-so-great accommodations.

As summer waned, we imagined our newly built home, and fun, exciting conversations filled our time and hearts.

It still seemed like we were behind in the normal development of a family after "hanging on" and "figuring it out" for years. Our progress felt unique because most families don't usually deal with the kind of hardships we faced, especially so early in a marriage.

Building a new home represented the next chapter in our lives and marked another part of our evolving perspective. For the first time, I felt like we were like everyone else as we fulfilled this goal—moving into a planned, accessible home.

This move wasn't a reaction to an unplanned event or tragedy; our new home symbolized progress and a good life.

Home

The extremes of emotion, sensation, and belief that began with that cold night in November deeply affected our lives. I didn't believe I could atone for my life. And then, in a blur of emotional peaks and valleys, while our hearts healed, we were waiting one morning to start the next chapter. We fought through disbelief. And this cathartic victory assured us of our combined strengths.

Suddenly, moving day was here. With our crumpled checklist discarded, we were finally moving in. Unlike the days and months after my accident, our emotions were soaring. Many had supported us through the darkest times when our lives were forever altered. And now they were here to help us move into our new home—a stark contrast. A close friend offered her truck to transport our belongings from The Mouse House to our new place. Family members and friends pitched in too. While some loaded the vehicles, others waiting at our house offered ideas for landscaping the yard, decorating the patio, and building storage in the garage.

The inaccessibility of our old brick home dulled any joyful, move-in moments. At this house, waiting for our belongings and savoring the excitement of a fresh start—wandering through empty rooms, lying on the new carpet making snow angels—we were celebrating sacrifices, fulfilled dreams, and answered prayers. We were overjoyed.

A U-Haul truck eventually showed up with most of the large items. While the helpers started unpacking boxes, Sylvia excitedly switched her attention to direct traffic, telling the guys where to place the washer and dryer, couches, beds, and my environmental control unit. It happened in a whirlwind. The boxes, clothes, dishes, and food were sorted and placed in their rooms with people in and out. Then, after the heavy lifting, the guys migrated to the driveway where they played on Jacob's basketball hoop. At the end of the day, everyone enjoyed pizza. Sylvia and I couldn't help but wear Cheshire cat-like smiles after things settled. Moving was everything we hoped it would be.

The following morning, our senses worked overtime with new home smells like fresh paint, new carpet, and fresh-cut lumber. Bare walls, canvasses that needed artwork, waited for our touch of personality. That defiant feeling of being someplace you weren't supposed to be, but you crashed the party anyway, added to the mood for me. I felt like I cheated to get here. A small part of me didn't feel deserving. But this was for all of us. I wanted this for Jacob and Sylvia. We all shared in the rush.

The following morning, the house was still in a state of disarray and many of our items were yet to be unpacked. However, Sylvia had set aside my new shower sling in anticipation of the first shower I would have in years. She also located our towels and bathing supplies as we discussed how to proceed.

Anticipation swelled in me as Sylvia moved about. I could tell she was excited for me as she searched with a purpose, retrieving the Hoyer lift and straps and unused shower items I had received 10 years before. I began thinking about years of bed baths from aides, too many to count. Having a bed bath to clean my body every day served a purpose. However, they aren't the same as a shower. I didn't *need* a shower since the bed bath cleaned my body. But knowing I could have one if it were only accessible often evoked despair. Sometimes I dreamed of looking up to meet the spray of a shower on my face.

After locating what we needed, Sylvia placed the shower sling under me. She briefly stepped out to inform Jacob that we would be busy for a little while. Then she returned and wheeled the Hoyer and me into the accessible bathroom to get started. Reflecting, I looked around and realized I hadn't been in a personal bathroom for a long time. After lifting over the threshold of the shower, she rolled me in and turned the water on to warm it up. I wasn't in the warmth of the spray all the way yet, but I could barely keep it together as Sylvia prepared to shower with me. I'd spent so much time pining for this. Holding back my emotions proved difficult. It was like a 5-year-old, unable to buy candy his entire childhood, frequenting a candy store with his allowance in his pocket.

Before she stepped in, Sylvia checked the temperature of the water one more time. She positioned the Hoyer so that the warm, comforting spray covered my body. And as she adjusted the shower curtains and slid into place with me, I closed my eyes—taking in the significance. I felt so incredibly gratified. I had taken so many things for granted—even during the years I examined my life after the accident. I'd wanted this so much. And it was finally happening after almost a decade.

Supported by a sling that allowed me to hang in this perfect space, my heart was overwhelmed. I looked up at Sylvia when she asked how I was. Like tears in the rain, the shower concealed the moment's impact—and my understanding of fairness—as Sylvia and I felt closer with each passing second. She shampooed my hair, washed my body, and then shampooed and washed hers.

As time went on, our routine would vary at times—sometimes getting showers from aides.

But the best part of my day was when Sylvia and I shared these morning showers. We connected and communicated before life started.

There were other consequences directly related to the daily showers. They kept my lungs and skin atypically healthy—especially for a C3 quad—so skin breakdowns weren't something I had to deal with. The daily experience also buoyed my mental outlook. And obstacles and difficulties inherent in a disabled life seemed smaller—all because of a simple shower.

As we finished unpacking during the days and weeks that followed, Sylvia and I began discussing what we wanted for the next chapter of our lives. It was still a fun way to build on a relationship that grew from heartache. Sylvia was eager to add our personality and belongings to our new home, begin a new modality at work, and exercise to be as healthy as possible.

Jacob was thrilled in a new room, playing in the yard with his dog, Nina, and continuing to play sports and learn music. I always wanted to give back as much as I've received. Helping Jacob and Sylvia was validating as they were my focus. My other plans for a positive future weren't grand. They included creating a small space at the new home to continue exploring art's influence in my life and discovering the possibilities of the accessible backyard. I had a place to love, teach, paint, and give back. And I could have a shower!

A home is a place that holds your belongings—sentimental items that describe your interests and personality. The place that starts your day, keeps you and your loved ones safe at night, and gives you a sense of security. We looked forward to making memories and growing here—having get-togethers and parties, finding ways to participate and adapt, and planning for the future. And as we adapted our uniqueness to embrace these very typical goals, we continued setting aside the pain.

Gaining Confidence

The encouraging effect of our home extended to other places. One of the best influences on my personal growth and confidence at this time was my participation in the local Junior Golf Association. Working with junior golfers allowed me to reimagine a pastime I used to enjoy. As I searched for ways to participate, volunteering and helping with the program in any way I could, golf gave me back a level of self-confidence I had been missing. The golf course surprisingly became a source of well-being and accomplishment.

From the first golf interactions when Jacob confused a two-inch tap-in as a "migge" instead of a "gimme," I participated vicariously and would go on to engage local businesses, organize playdays, and encourage the golfers of the Caldwell Junior Golf Association for the next decades. My involvement has been one of the most uplifting stories of my life.

Art, Part of a Steady Trend Since Childhood

I wasn't good at doodling as a young boy, but I enjoyed it. As I got older, all the time spent learning music, playing baseball and football, and trying to make sense of life's lessons didn't leave room for anything else. So I soon forgot about drawing just for fun.

Then, I rediscovered art after I became a quadriplegic. Art became part of the milieu of perseverance, a bright spot in a very dark and ominous time. I found hope in art—in its connection to the past, present, and future. However, my psychological progress didn't improve my physical health. My disabled body remained frail—possibly forever. I couldn't do anything taxing for more than three or four hours without my body reacting negatively. Still, I could sketch for short periods with my easel and rest when needed—a compromise.

The fact that I had to learn on my own was a blessing in disguise. There was no tutorial (no YouTube) about how to draw or paint with your mouth. So, learning to create art—how to do what others do with their hands—with my mouth was a way to pass the time and keep depression in the box of worries. Searching for ways to adapt was an unexpected source of therapy that helped fill gaps in my new life—a small win.

Then, I started visiting Elks Rehabilitation Hospital to add more meaning to my life. Art helped pave the way to reach patients as cracks in my confidence began smoothing over. I didn't notice that art influenced parts of almost everything in my life at one time or another: my emotions, family, patients I visited at Elks, places I went to, and the way I saw the world. Learning to draw with my mouth was one of the reasons I healed—a new me. Even when I was young, the arts in general—music, drawing, dancing, and literature—set an unlikely foundation, a starting point, to build from.

Years later, I met Dave, an accomplished painter who introduced me to watercolor while we were at an art show with George. Dave's humor, generosity, and talent made talking to him easy. And after a few visits to get to know each other, he offered to give me 20-minute painting lessons during shows we attended. Another piece of the puzzle fell into place with his selfless gesture to teach me.

Dave and I quickly became friends as he hinted at new possibilities for my future—for my growing confidence and evolution. Each time we saw each other, he would show me how he used his mouth, practicing at home, to find techniques I could use. It was comical to see him demonstrate since he wore dentures. But he was a good sport anyway. Eventually, the idea of painting gave me confidence enough to buy brushes, paints, and color wheels. And I read books and researched watercolor art to learn as much as I could about painting.

Adding color to my palette was metaphorical—a transition from a black-and-white world as I added color to my life. After we moved into our shower-accessible home, I began gathering paints, brushes, and tools needed for my art room. As I collected everything, I felt a sense of accomplishment—a feeling of well-being like when you receive an award or are given a compliment. In retrospect, it's hard to believe my perspective was so affected by such an unlikely source.

Looking back, the tenor of my life began trending up for me long before I understood it was. The progress in my art room started years ago when I was young. My father's influence—the dysfunction of adolescence that caused doubt and worry—might have remained an emotional wound into adulthood, but coping with hardship at a young age nurtured resilience and determination, not just sadness. Resilience born of a challenging situation is a part of who I am. Childhood heartache indirectly prepared me for a disabled life years later. And it took my accident to see my father's influence wasn't all sad—that he is still a part of me.

Life improving after my accident started with Sylvia's strength and the support of family and friends. The trend continued with a respiratory therapist at Rancho, a return home, and the easel George gave me. We withstood another accident, more doubt, and kicks to the face. And we arrived at this physical and emotional place where we could be thankful for the struggle. Even our playful labrador Nina—who loved wallowing into the ditch and became excited about cows in the neighboring field—helped me see that I actually did have the "white picket fence."

NINA

Sometimes Nina would chill with me in the living room or in the garage when weather permitted—protective. I think she had a sense of my broken body, my need for help. With Jacob, Sylvia, and everyone else, Nina was like the "bull in the China shop"—a big, 100-pound lab. With me, however, she was uncannily gentle. Nina would climb next to me on Sylvia's bed and rest her head on my chest without placing any weight on me as if she knew. And she would balance on her hind legs to place her paws on my forearm as I sat in my wheelchair—without putting any weight on my arm. Nina had also successfully protected our family in the past. She would stay close to me when I was outside, watching over me. As much as a pet understands frailty, she understood me.

One afternoon, Nina and I were alone in the living room listening to music. Sylvia was leaving to pick up Jacob from a function he was at. And before she left, she asked if I needed anything and then ushered Nina outside since she hadn't been out for a while. We dismissed the clouds rolling in because they wouldn't be gone very long. I might have heard the low rumble of thunder if I hadn't been rocking out to my music.

The storm we had ignored soon enveloped our home like a stealthy assassin—bringing severe rain, thunder, and lightning. When the first visible flash of lightning produced its ominous crack, I realized I had failed.

Nina ran to the door—expecting me to respond. She visibly grew more frightened, cowering with each flash of lightning and crack of thunder while my helpless heart sank. She pressed her body to the door—urging me to open it. But all I could do was yell through the glass door. "Hold on Nina, they'll be back." I was reassuring myself more than anything. She didn't understand my abandonment. But I wanted her to hear my voice to console her until they returned. The seconds were like hours as she trembled and pawed at the threshold—as the storm's intensity increased.

While she leaned against the door's glass pane to get as close to me as she could—to permeate through, she was asking for my help with her big brown eyes. But I couldn't. The roar became so unbearable that she began gnawing at the door frame to try and help herself—bloodying her mouth. But all I could do was apologize as I yelled over and over. "I'm sorry, Nina! I'm sorry, Nina!" I hadn't felt this incapable and useless for some time. The most intense part of the storm only lasted 20 or 30 minutes—the entire time it took Sylvia and Jacob to return home. It felt like forever.

Despair stained each solemn word as I explained what happened during the storm. I told Sylvia I felt responsible while they consoled our lovable Lab and me. Sylvia said, over and over, "She's okay, babe. Look, she's okay." To her credit and forgiving appeal, Nina wagged her tail with each reassuring hug.

What Nina and I shared was unexpected and painful. But the moment shifted away from those initial feelings of helplessness because she recovered so well. Everything was back to usual hours later. I counted my blessings.

Nina helped me move on like only a loving dog could. I didn't want to look back and wish I had done things differently—especially since Sylvia and Jacob fed off how I reacted to situations that could be challenging and awkward.

Choosing to smile continued to be my internal mantra. Just like Nina's wagging tail, I could share a friendly smile or wink to affect everyone around me.

Color in My Life

Worries about limitations to access the yard, rooms, and shower weren't front and center anymore. They were replaced by considerations for building an art room and all that entailed: having an accessible easel, finding a way to reach paint and water with a mouth stick, and how to light my area were just a few of the welcome obstacles I was eager to overcome. Accomplishing these things provided a reward that felt more substantial—like getting a toy for your eighth birthday instead of socks.

Eventually, with the tools, supplies, and confidence to begin, I created a method to paint with a caregiver's help. The process of gathering all I needed peaked. A week later, with Dave's voice in my head, I finished my first watercolor. Art became one of the most enjoyable challenges for me to overcome. Ultimately, Dave's lessons and advice—not to be afraid to try novel things—helped me dive into the next phase of my life.

My first attempts to paint with my mouth seemed difficult at first. I soon realized, however, that art wasn't about perfection, or a specific standard outlined in a particular book somewhere. Art and creating it was about expressing what I saw and what I felt. That meant I could appreciate art and admire it like everyone else. Being disabled doesn't affect my perception of what art is or if a painting or a sketch I've done is any good. It just affects the way I produce it.

The relationship between art, George, and my personal development, along with its positive impact on my family, inspired me to maintain my health, leave the house, and foster positive change while reducing self-blame. Visiting the hospital became extremely rewarding as I formed meaningful relationships with patients, staff, and George. Through these experiences, I no longer felt insignificant; instead, I began to see how a disabled life could be fulfilling and even joyful—in part because of my new-found pastime.

Life isn't defined by the big, grand occasions sprinkled throughout our past. Instead, it is defined by seemingly insignificant moments when we teach, show compassion and love, and give a little of ourselves to others.

In a special moment, my niece Michelle contributed to one of these special, life-defining moments. My sisters' kids came over often to play with Jacob and help with things I couldn't do. I don't recall why Michelle, my sister's youngest, was there that day. But we were alone for a moment when I noticed her untied shoes and asked her to tie them so she wouldn't trip and fall. Despite being a preschooler, she was attentive and fun to be around. So, I was curious how she would respond.

Michelle looked up at me with her usual grin and responded, "I don't know how, Tio." I reflexively chimed in, "Do you want to learn? I'll teach you." She was only four. And my response was part of my evolving confidence because I was unsure how I would teach her even this simple task. Not surprisingly, Michelle promptly nodded with a mischievous smile. All of her siblings had been helpful to me, positively reacting to my wheelchair. And Michelle seemed to know more than her age would suggest. Over the years, I figured out how to live and find my way. So, why couldn't I teach her?

Her playful reaction made me laugh out loud. I asked. "What do you know how to do?" Michelle carefully showed me she could make a loop and wrap a lace around the loop. But she was unsure what to do next. So I started from the beginning. I explained. "Cross the laces, one over the other, then wrap under again and pull." She semi-knew that part. "Now, make a loop on one side. Take the long lace on the other side and wrap it around the loop. Then, push the loose end through the hole." She followed instructions well for a 4-year-old and helped me as I helped her. Back and forth we went— "This hole, Tio?"

"Nope."
"This hole?"
"Nope."
"This hole?"

"Yep, yep, yep," I said. (We both liked Ducky from *The Land Before Time*.) "Now, pull through."

I explained every motion, every tuck and pull of a lace for 15 minutes as she listened closely. When she accomplished each correct next step, we backtracked and repeated, connecting them into a sequence. And after a bit of practice, she figured it out. We laughed out loud as she stared at her accomplishment—because "Tio Non" taught her to tie her shoes.

Teaching my niece was an inconsequential 10 or 15 minutes of my time. And I had my doubts. But it felt great when Michelle and I told her siblings about the new skill she learned. They were also surprised and thought it was pretty awesome—big, big win!

We had more wins and defeats—enough of each to stop keeping count. And our evolving perspective helped remind us that we need to focus on the wins—the bits of life that make us smile and appreciate each other.

To some degree, everyone deals with hardship during their lifetime. It also seems like some don't struggle at all. And it's futile to debate fairness because people who struggle react to suffering and sorrow differently. I can't say that my life is more challenging than someone who has lost a family member, gone through a divorce, or dealt with cancer. Pain and loss are subjective. *Everyone* hurts.

But the tears, worries, pain, and hardship we experienced over the 10 years after my accident seemed more than most. At the other end of the emotional spectrum, we dreamed of a daughter. I told myself that hoping for a miracle wasn't selfish despite feeling guilty for wanting and praying for something so monumental.

The first step toward becoming parents again came when Sylvia reached out to her doctor, expressing our desire for a daughter. His response was both heartening and unexpected—his confident and reassuring demeanor easing much of the doubt and anxiety we had accumulated over the years. As we continued to discuss the possibilities, Dr. Schaeffer's unwavering optimism only strengthened our growing hope.

The first hurdle we faced was an evaluation of Sylvia's and my health. We were anxious because both possible outcomes—good or bad—meant big changes in our outlook. But the result was that my health, atypical for a quad, and Sylvia's health checked out. We started truly imagining what the future with another child would be like. It fueled our hearts.

A happy nervousness kept us on edge, feeling vulnerable during this time. But we grew closer through our emotions and feelings because of this shared dream. And after several exciting months of trying, it happened.

Chapter 10

Our Daughter

The notion that you can predict your future is naive and self-indulgent. Of course you can't. But when you're young and start dating someone you can imagine a life with, you begin to picture a possible future painted with picket fences and a dog named Fido. When Sylvia's and my relationship was brand new, I hoped for a fairytale ending. Even though I was apprehensive about commitment, my heart wanted this.

However, life doesn't usually turn out how you imagined it. Everything we planned and hoped for early in the romance flew out the window when the accident happened. There was no chance for me to address problems caused by my insecurities and work on our young relationship. A happy ending vanished.

Our thoughts and emotions were all over the place as we dealt with an uncertain future. We struggled to see anything worth fighting for. We couldn't imagine the home, the planned children, or the silly dog.

Then, we began a slow climb out of the darkness. Each impediment on our path provided friction to gain traction and move forward. And the slow advance and accumulated small wins added to our psyche to imagine a future. They helped us stay the course when we couldn't see one. Through the storm and uncertainty, we found gratitude for a good life. Despite the odds, we remained optimistic as we gathered information and tried to conceive. Life was exciting again.

Then, an unbelievable lightning strike changed everything. After all the difficulties of the last 13 years, hearing that we were pregnant was more than a surprise. The news was validating, redeeming, and a dream realized for Sylvia, Jacob, and me. I challenged the idea of fairness and equity for a long time without resolution. News that we were expecting helped even a lopsided equation for me. Experiences that led us to this moment, many of them gut-wrenching, prepared us to take on the next challenge of raising a child.

With our hearts overflowing with renewed hope, we eagerly shifted our focus toward the tangible reality of welcoming our baby into the world. Every day became a flurry of preparations—from assembling the perfect nursery to ensuring our home was safe and welcoming for our new addition. As we discussed baby names and speculated about potential personality traits, our conversations were punctuated by happy, teary-eyed smiles, each exchange filled with anticipation for the unexpected joys and milestones that awaited us. In those moments, we could already envision the sound of joyful giggles filling our home and the precious memories we would create together.

As we prepared for the arrival of our new baby, one concern weighed heavily on our minds—how would Jacob react to having a sibling? We worried that amidst the excitement of a new addition, he might feel overshadowed or left out. However, our fears were alleviated when we finally shared the news with him. His eyes lit up with a mixture of surprise and joy, tears came, but his smile told the whole story. In that moment, any doubts or uncertainties vanished, replaced by a profound sense of relief and gratitude. Jacob's genuine excitement not only affirmed our decision to expand our family, it also filled our hearts with anticipation for the beautiful journey that lay ahead.

Thinking about the relevance of our unorthodox journey, we also didn't want to dismiss the pain, the mountains we climbed, and the lessons we learned because they had shaped us in profound ways—strengthening our bond and our determination, indirectly preparing us for the challenges ahead. Struggles and the perseverance they nurture are part of who we are—and the emotional bond that grew from them helped us prepare mentally for this moment. The lessons we learned along the way became guiding lights, illuminating our path forward with resilience and confidence.

As Sylvia's pregnancy progressed, her life underwent a profound transformation, both physically and psychologically. The unique routines of our environment that had become familiar since the accident gave way to a whole new set of experiences and sensations. Physically, she found herself navigating the distant memories of pregnancy-related changes—following a carefully crafted nutrition plan, supplementing with vitamins, and grappling with unpredictable cravings and aversions. Each day brought its own set of surprises as her body adapted to the demands of pregnancy.

Sylvia had terrible morning sickness that began shortly after conception. She spent the majority of the first trimester queasy—dry-heaving into a towel, often by simply thinking about specific foods or driving the van. It was an exhausting period that continued for some time.

Alongside these physical changes, I also observed shifts in Sylvia's psyche. She approached her renewed role with a blend of excitement and apprehension, eagerly preparing for the future while grappling with the uncertainties that lay ahead. One noticeable change was her meticulous attention to cleanliness, as she found herself compulsively cleaning and organizing every corner of our home. While initially surprising, I understood that this behavior was a manifestation of her nesting instinct—a natural urge to create a safe and welcoming environment for our growing family.

Despite the challenges and uncertainties of what a pregnancy meant for me as a disabled parent, I found solace in witnessing Sylvia's happiness and determination. Her neurotic tendencies, once a source of amusement, now served as a testament to her unwavering commitment to our family's well-being. As we embarked on this new chapter together, I was reminded of Sylvia's resilience and strength over the years, knowing that whatever challenges lay ahead, we would face them together, united in love and anticipation for the future.

Other fun detours in our evolving situation included changes to our weekend routines while picking up groceries and lunch, as well as unplanned visits to Babies 'R' Us. In addition, we talked about whether the baby might learn piano like his big brother and what sports they might be interested in. The entire experience was fun, exciting, and chaotic.

Our lives, abundant with the extremes of emotion, high and low, reached a crescendo of joy when we discovered during a prenatal ultrasound that we were having a baby girl. I closed my eyes and danced like in my dreams, thanking God for her. The late-night conversations Sylvia and I shared more than a decade earlier had accomplished so much more than helping soothe our wounded spirits during the most trying and emotional period of our lives. Thirteen years later, this miracle, born of those distant conversations, achieved something so unlikely. And gave us the momentum to keep going.

We managed our excitement enough to keep our families in the dark, unaware of our godsend. We didn't want to tempt fate and jinx ourselves. However, they sensed something was different about us. It may have been the typical glow exuded by a happy mother-to-be or a change in Sylvia's appetite that tipped them off. Maybe they could sense the giddy excitement I carried under the surface.

One example of the possibility that our family knew about the pregnancy was our 4-year-old niece who was obsessed with Sylvia's belly. Somehow, she sensed something. And a few of our family members gave us what seemed like lopsided smiles for a while. Still, we waited to tell all of them until we were confident there wouldn't be any setbacks, deciding to share the news at Christmas before someone guessed.

When we finally revealed our secret to our family, everyone was elated, overwhelming us with their response. Their joyous reaction—happy tears, big hugs, and curious questions—reminded us of how unique and special a baby was for us. I still felt internal anxiety as a disabled parent as we shared the news with them—as I had throughout the pregnancy. But I was as happy as I had ever been in the last 13 years.

Well into the pregnancy, Sylvia was changing daily as she was driven to clean obsessively, and eat spicy foods, typical hormone-driven behavior. It wasn't long before we had a crib, baby blankets, and a small dresser to furnish the baby's room. We also bought and washed baby clothes—so my wife could take deep breaths while burying her face in them—and organized them in pink drawers. And Sylvia decorated the walls with balloons and rainbows. The crib was given to her by a friend and it had a pink mobile.

Sylvia continued receiving daily pick-me-ups from her hospital friends as we counted the days until our daughter's birthday. The consistency and friendships that came with participating in sports and school kept Jacob happy and content. Meanwhile, I felt content as I continued volunteering at the hospital, giving back, encouraging patients if I could. And, despite losing my space to a nursery, I also painted more, finding unique ways to create with my mouth. As anticipation grew, we prepared for what lay ahead.

While the expected June due date quickly approached, we began checking off things that are necessary for a baby's arrival. Getting a car seat installed, baby-proofing the house, and packing a bag for the hospital, we hoped to sidestep any unwanted mishaps.

The last week of May came quickly. Even so, we thought we had a little time to finish fully preparing for the birth of our daughter. However, she decided she wasn't waiting for that to happen.

Caught off guard when Sylvia's water unexpectedly broke one morning—weeks before her scheduled due date—instant chaos ensued. We hadn't entirely put the logistics of bringing a baby into this world in place. This included figuring out who could take Sylvia to the hospital. Failing to prepare mentally by doing tai chi or reading the baby books we were supposed to added to the chaos. Although we had done well up to this point, we had procrastinated—usually my MO. Isabella was coming, and we had to focus. We had to prepare our emotions, expectations, and hearts for this life-changing event.

The impact of my accident altered every part of who we were. For Sylvia, thinking about having a baby after my injury might have felt a little selfish—like it was for me—because so many aspects of our lives were unknown. She'd put herself second while focusing on loving someone with a disability. Sure, she took weekend trips with wonderful friends and appreciated them. They helped her get away from duty. But the trips seemed a compromise for the grand family trip we never took. Traveling without Jacob and me also tore at her heart. She often mentioned that she wished I could go with her—my burden staining her excursions as well. For a long time, she had no expectations of our lives being blessed with this moment. Having another baby was truly the greatest blessing.

After the excited conversation about the evolving situation, Sylvia and I came to our senses. Shifting gears, beginning with a quick shower, Sylvia got dressed and gathered the baby bag and necessary clothes. She was a little concerned that I wouldn't be at the hospital since my caregiver wasn't there yet. But I reassured her as she hurried about. I told her that everything would work out like we imagined as I reached out to my caregiver friend. I also attempted to contact my sister to drive Sylvia to the hospital, to no avail—adding more angst to an emotionally hectic situation.

The mood calmed a second while Sylvia finished preparing. Becky, my caregiver, returned my call, letting me know she was on her way to help me into my wheelchair so I could meet my daughter. However, she mentioned it would take some time for her to arrive. As Sylvia and I anxiously waited, the seconds seemed to stretch into eternity. The flurry of activity was replaced by an intense stillness, making those few minutes the most nerve-wracking part of the morning.

Sylvia kept glancing at the clock, her worry growing with each passing moment. I tried to keep her calm, assuring her that Becky would arrive soon and everything would be alright. But despite my reassurances, the tension was palpable.

Finally, it became clear that waiting for my sister wasn't a viable option. Sylvia couldn't wait any longer. Under protest, she grabbed her bag and left, a mixture of determination and anxiety in her eyes. As she hurried out, I felt a pang of guilt for not being able to accompany her, but I knew she had to go.

Just a few minutes later, my sister walked in the front door. "Sylvia are you here?" she called out. She laughed when I shook my head and told her Sylvia had left impatiently just three minutes before. There was no way she could catch Sylvia before she reached the hospital. Sylvia's focus was on having the baby. Still, my sister hurried out to be there for her.

When Becky finally arrived, we skipped my daily shower and she helped me into my wheelchair. Then we speedily made our way to the hospital—the regularly granny-paced drive replaced by a body-lurching 20 minutes. The drive felt farther than normal, each minute stretching longer as my mind raced with thoughts of Sylvia and the baby.

When we finally got to the hospital, I was rushed to the delivery room. I saw my wife waiting with Dr. Schaeffer for me to arrive so they could continue. The room buzzed with anticipation, and my heart raced as I prepared to meet our daughter. Sylvia spoke, a mixture of relief and joy in her voice. We were finally ready for this moment.

The context of our daughter's birth was vastly different from our son's. Sylvia and I were more mentally prepared this time because we had been through it before. With Jacob, I had taken much of the first baby experience for granted. I was naive and didn't fully appreciate the gift of parenthood. Surviving my crash, discovering a renewed purpose, finding the will to live, and then rekindling my relationship with Sylvia and Jacob prepared my heart for a baby girl. This time, the understanding and wisdom we had gained made all the difference.

When Dr. Schaeffer brought her into the world, Isabella had a full head of dark black hair like Don King. She was tiny and seemed almost unreal. When she cried as the nurse held her, I cried too, overwhelmed by the depth of my emotions. Sylvia's close friends and co-workers stood at the door, equally moved. Not forgetting our son, they quickly alerted the school to let Jacob know he was now a big brother.

Izzy's arrival marked another shift from heartache to hope, from sorrow to love. She was more than a symbol of our perseverance; she breathed new life into our world.

Her birth was a testament to the love and dedication we shared—a symbol of hope, the kind that guided us through the darkest times.

Now, each milestone she reached, each smile she graced us with, reaffirmed the bond that held us together, reminding us of the incredible journey we had undertaken as a family.

The weeks flew by as we adjusted to a schedule revolving around our adorable baby girl. The changes were both comforting and daunting, affecting everyone in the family. I worried, not in a bad way, that a new addition might alter what we had built over the years. But Sylvia was a rock star, taking care of Isabella's needs with unwavering dedication. Jacob needed me to be as committed a father as possible as he shared the spotlight. To his credit and my relief, he was a thoughtful and loving big brother, holding Izzy often and doing all the things big brothers do.

My self-perceived inadequacy waxed and waned as I observed Sylvia and Jacob seamlessly meeting all of Izzy's needs. For every milestone we approached, I was determined to help in any way I could, understanding that I could be her daddy.

Inspiration led to solutions as I constantly looked for ways to be involved. For instance, over the years, I understood that Sylvia, in her bed next to mine, felt my movements at night. Years of spasms and the occasional, "Did you hear that, Mama?" at three in the morning kept Sylvia half awake. These movements were counterproductive at times, but I could also use them to rock Izzy to sleep. It was a workout as I made the sh-sh-sh sound and moved my head like a crazed person shaking a bee out of my hair to coax her to sleep. I could rock Izzy while in my chair, but I loved this goofy approach too.

Baby schedules these first few months were exhausting, learning all over again how to care for a newborn. No sooner had we found a rhythm than Sylvia's maternity leave came to an end—with one weekend left to prepare for a new schedule.

The predicament—Izzy was three months old and still refused the bottle, insisting on nursing. For Sylvia to return to work, Izzy had to make the switch. After a frantic weekend of trying, she finally cooperated, and the Calsen's daycare gave us peace of mind.

Unlike the shock of the past, we had planned for this, knowing I couldn't care for her the way an able-bodied parent could. But I found solace in knowing the Calsen's were there for us—just as they had been when Jacob grew up in the same environment.

We weren't off-balance anymore, afraid of the future. I didn't worry when someone else cared for her while I spent the day with my caregiver. Being alone had its upside. It gave me the space to focus on my goals—art, volunteerism, and exploring ways to further support my family.

As we watched Izzy grow into a happy, curly-haired, daring little girl, it was irresistible to compare the similarities and differences between her and her brother. We couldn't have imagined the blessing they would become. But we COULD imagine saying to Jacob, "Be nice to your sister," or "Share with your brother"—conversations I never expected for a decade, considering the obstacles we had to overcome. I felt overwhelming joy thinking about every new day.

Their individual personalities provided two opportunities for us to grow and learn as parents and people. We noticed Izzy liked pink and watching *Dora the Explorer*, and she was sillier and more playful than her brother. Funny enough, she also had more of a temper than her big brother too. Considering these personality differences made us happy because we were in an emotionally positive place.

All parents use a lens of love and care to navigate their children's differences, but for us, the perspective was shaped by the concern of raising them in a disabled environment. For me, more than I wanted to admit.

From our viewpoint, Izzy's response to her environment was entirely typical, given its atypical nature. With a disabled father being all she'd ever known, she had nothing to compare her situation to. The effects of growing up in a unique environment went unnoticed because her life didn't begin with the confusion and heartache that Jacob's did. Her reaction to the wheelchair, caregivers, and adapted home was almost dismissive—in the best way possible.

Jacob, on the other hand, experienced an emotional climate that was anything but typical. He witnessed the drastic changes brought by my accident and tried to manage his emotions, often asking how *we* were, concerned that *we* were alright. His personality is more reserved than his sister's, but there's no question that his experience shaped him. The compassion he displays is that of an old soul, seemingly nurtured by the challenges he faced early on.

In the end, I'm grateful that they're happy, knowing my mistakes didn't affect them as much as I once feared they might. Each has their own unique gifts and personality. Beyond their response to having a disabled father, I've cherished the distinctive interactions and perspectives that quadriplegia has imposed on them.

I coached them both in the only way I knew how. When Jacob was 10, I recorded a video of Tim Hardaway, the NBA legend known for his killer crossover dribble. We would watch and discuss the move—how Hardaway would lean to bait his defender and how Jacob could replicate it by becoming equally adept with both hands. We talked about strategy—keeping your body between the defender and the ball. Jacob absorbed what he learned and became a better player, offensively and defensively.

Similarly, I used YouTube to teach Izzy soccer skills. We watched videos together, learning how to make defenders lean one way, use feints, and utilize the outside of the feet as much as the inside. I also used magazines to show her the proper shaft position and wrist angle at the top of her golf swing, the forward shaft lean at impact, and the correct grip. The technique I used with her was similar to the one I used with Jacob—relying on videos and images to replace the physical demonstrations I couldn't perform myself.

Revisiting the differences in their reactions to my coaching is still a joy. As I stare out the window, smiling, I find myself reliving those moments—the times when I was more involved in their lives than I ever thought possible.

Take Izzy, for example. Her fiery response to a frustrating practice session often led to intense conversations. She'd demand, "Why aren't you fixing my shanks?" or exclaim, "Are you going to help me or not?" Her determination was fierce, especially when she'd say, "I have to beat her! So I need to fix this. Are you watching?" It was humorous, that fire in her.

Jacob, on the other hand, grew more reserved as he got older—perhaps because boys are often simpler creatures. Saying that Jacob was typical because he liked sports might be an over-generalization but give a 10-year-old boy a ball and some food, and he's usually content. That was Jacob. Though, both he and Izzy shared a fondness for the clubhouse French fries after a round of golf.

Watching their personalities evolve was a gift I hadn't imagined I'd have—the chance to look back on my life as a quadriplegic parent and savor those moments. When Izzy was born, she healed parts of my heart that had remained broken because I could no longer hold my son. She helped me piece together my shattered confidence, reminding me that what I'd done for Jacob wasn't just a fluke—a reminder that doubt is a constant companion in the mind of someone living with a disability.

UNDERSTANDING

Over time, I understood that Jacob was quieter than Izzy—more reserved because of his personality. Of course, he was affected by my accident. However, I could stop kicking myself whenever he acted reserved. His lack of expressed anger toward me was, in part, personality—not just concern for a disabled dad.

During practice, Izzy paid little attention to everything else—like my inabilities. Instead, she concentrated on a goal she was working toward. I felt relieved—in a way—because she didn't worry that I might need shade. After all, I could overheat. Smiling, Izzy would remind me to drink water, but she wouldn't stop practicing to get the drink for me. She understands that my caregiver helps me. Her perspective is that I am healthy. I am a regular dad who shows her how to do stuff. So, I feel she wasn't affected by my accident the way Jacob was.

The effect of my disability on my family will always be a concern for me. Shedding my insecurities—the emotional baggage I carry—has been an ongoing process that is present more than it should be. I still wonder how they feel about me missing out—especially when I am too tired to stay in my wheelchair longer than 10 or 11 hours to do something later in the evening. Am I less of a father or husband than other dads or husbands? Have I harmed them because I can't protect them with a strong arm or go somewhere that isn't planned? I don't want to admit that I still carry guilt, fear, and worry. However, I eventually realized they were okay. My children taught me that a disabled parent can be everything any other parent can be.

Added Perspective

When Jacob was 11, he entered an essay contest with the prompt, "Someone you admire, your hero." His essay, titled "Life Without My Mom Would Be Much Harder," was a heartfelt tribute to Sylvia. From his young perspective, Jacob wrote about her strength and everything she had done for our family in the years following my life-altering accident. It was heartbreaking that his understanding of what we'd been through was surprisingly mature beyond his years, a sad reflection of the challenges we had overcome.

In contrast, when Izzy wrote a similar essay as a young teen, her perspective was different. Her essay carried an idealistic tone, focusing on the unique advantages of having a disabled father, rather than the emotional hardships.

Her paper:

> *"Faster! Faster!" I'd yell, smiling, hanging on from the back of my dad's wheelchair as the forward motion of his chin control fabricated the very impetus of my character. From our kitchen to the living room, to the aisles of the grocery store, my innocent psyche screamed at the world around me with every escape of laughter. Twelve years prior to my birth, my father sustained a life-threatening car accident that left him completely paralyzed from the neck down. No longer able to do things like feed and bathe himself, the thought of being a husband and a father was an unfathomable notion. This instance would change my mother's and brother's life in a matter of seconds, but for me this was a normality. From the time I was born, adaptation was an innate gift bestowed upon me bound by the cost of having a disabled father.*
>
> *Adaptation was uniquely built into the foundation of my childhood home, as it had been designed with ramps and wide doorways for accessibility. My auditory senses were at odds with society as I learned to listen to the clicks of my dad's wheelchair rather than the weight of his footsteps, and I would create bonds with the various caretakers that exhausted their days in my home throughout my childhood. Similarly, I perfected cinematic masterpieces for student council using the swift movement of his wheelchair and enjoyed rides on the back of his wheelchair rather than his shoulders. Propitious, I left no room for people to question my optimism as I displayed the implications of my unique skill set.*

> *The latter developments affiliated with having a disabled parent, but rather my perfected adaptation, ensue relentless optimism, the appreciation for all things ordinary, the creativity to think of alternative solutions to plights in every walk of life, and the courage to exercise my adaptive creativity, none of which I would possess from the clarity that furnishes the lofty view over your dad's shoulders: wheelchair over piggyback.*

With the expansion of our family, I uncovered some fundamental truths about my role in it.

> *Parenting as a quadriplegic is different, but that's all it is—different.*

There is no right or wrong way to parent because of a disability, whether it's using a wheelchair, crutches, or dealing with visual impairment. What matters is that you parent with your heart. Over the years, Sylvia supported me through every doubt, reminding me that my disability didn't diminish their love for me.

My daughter was an unexpected joy in my new life, one of the final pieces of the puzzle that Sylvia and I had been putting together. Over time, my perspective shifted. I began to realize that the puzzle pieces in everyone's story are inherently incomplete. It's not about finding the perfect or ideal pieces. Some are torn, others are lost, and some no longer fit because life has reshaped them. But like any puzzle, when you step back—or wheel back—you can still see the full picture, even with the missing pieces. I hadn't realized that my life was already complete in its own way, but Izzy was the piece that brought the picture into clearer focus.

Chapter 11

Barefoot on the Green

I scrunched my feet on the fresh-cut grass, hoping to get a few holes in before dark. Sometimes after a round of golf, I would take my shoes off to let the dogs out and putt on the practice green to relax before I got in the car. In mid-summer, the cool grass contrasted with the hot weather. It was therapeutic to feel my toes free.

Eager to get out on the course, I walked over to the clubhouse to pay my green fees. However, the clubhouse was closed. That wasn't unusual, though. Now and then, they closed a bit early on a hot, dead, middle-of-the-week day. I hadn't laced up my golf shoes yet. And the thought of walking shoeless sounded pretty good. So, I called out one more time. "Hello. Is anyone here?"—to no avail. Since I enjoy 100-degree weather and the shop was closed, I decided to tee off—barefoot.

I placed my golf shoes back in the car. And then I grabbed my driver out of my bag, walked over to the tee box, and addressed the ball. It was such a nice day—alone with my thoughts. After I striped my drive right down the middle of the first fairway, I glanced around to see if someone might flash me a thumbs up. But I still hadn't seen ANYONE, not even a car. Disconcertingly, an uneasy feeling filled the air as I strode toward where my golf ball landed. I could always count on exercise and the sun on my face to feel better about myself. Spending time on the golf course was usually rejuvenating. However, the smells and sensations that normally evoked a sense of well-being—that pushed angst aside—were flat and numb. Instead, I felt detached trying to remember the last few months.

With each cool, barefoot step I took, faint memories of the past flickered like dying embers. Jacob, my usual golf buddy, was conspicuously absent. Each flex of my toes seemed to heighten the sense of his absence, as if my shoeless night somehow deepened the void he left behind. He had been gone for months, and the utter lack of any memory of him gnawed at me, a void that no solitary round of golf could ever fill. Anxious and disoriented, I struggled to recall a single moment of golfing with Jacob or teaching him the game. Why couldn't I remember? And then, more perplexingly, flashes of a curly-haired little girl invaded my consciousness, though I had no context for her presence.

Walking still felt pleasant as I approached the ball and paused to take a deep breath. Standing behind it, preparing for my next shot, I gauged the distance to the flag and decided on a three-quarter sand wedge. There was just enough daylight left for only three or four more holes. I wanted to make the most of the warm summer evening.

Pulling my club from the bag, I rehearsed my golf swing, remembering to limit my wrist flex during my pre-shot routine. I also tried to rationalize each confusing, out-of-place thought as I prepared, pausing for a second, still uneasy about the unusual quiet.

After dismissing the worry, the transition of my backswing felt good as I uncoiled and made solid contact. The ball listened and landed close enough to the flag for a birdie. I was acutely aware of the sweat collecting on my brow and how athletic and healthy I felt. The setting was perfect. But something was off. I couldn't put my finger on it.

While walking to the next hole barefoot, in shorts and a tank top, I felt a lonely desolation filling the edges of the golf course—almost as if I were part of an out-of-focus scene. Sylvia sometimes spent time golfing with me, but her absence now further heightened my sense of isolation.

There were other strange physical sensations as the night grew more confusing. Staring down at my bare feet as I walked, they seemed a long way from my body, like when you look at the ground for the first time with prescription glasses. Anxiety began to creep in like a lurking predator.

On the next hole, I also hit a nice short iron near the hole. And with each subsequent swing, I felt lonelier and lonelier instead of refreshed. I was desperate to hear a voice, anyone's. Following the second hole, I reached into my bag and grabbed a towel to wipe my face and a beer I'd stashed. I took a big drink and exhaled. But the reset I hoped to find at the course was absent. The evening, instead, was providing loneliness, consuming me.

Each swing now felt hollow, more uncertain than the last, the silence around me a constant reminder that I was out of place, not where I was supposed to be. But the sun on my face, the muscle-warming heat, and the act of walking kept me from giving in to the growing doubt.

I decided to skip to the last hole, not wanting to waste the walk back since it was on the way to my car. It also meant getting home sooner. And again, every shot I made was true. But the anxiety that had accumulated throughout the evening was now accompanied by physical pain. I was scared. There wasn't anyone to help explain the pain I felt in my body as I sat in the grass next to my car—no one to say "I don't feel right" to.

My shoes were in my bag. So, I unzipped the long zipper to retrieve them. They weren't there. Shaky, I lay back in the grass, closed my eyes, and tried to figure things out.

I abruptly opened my eyes as I felt the gagging irritation of a breathing tube reminding me I was in an all too familiar hospital. The sensations I felt—my body on fire, a pounding in my head, and complete and utter vulnerability—were intimate. My relationship with these places and services, where my health is maintained, is almost comforting because I have spent decades keeping the monsters away in this environment. Still, I felt disoriented and frightened.

But then I saw my wife next to my bed. I wasn't alone.

The nightmare was over.

I've come to realize that sometimes my brain plays out complex feelings in interesting ways, creating vivid, almost cinematic experiences as I navigate the ups and downs of health challenges. This dream was no exception, wrapping my emotions in a scene that felt so real it lingers even now. It's strange how the mind can take fragments of joy, fear, and longing, weaving them together into something that feels alive. This one still feels incredibly vivid to this day, a reminder of the strange and beautiful complexity of how we process the challenges life throws at us.

Chapter 12

A Better Understanding

Painting, volunteering, and participating as much as possible, my life fell into a comfortable groove. Wounds and heartache that piled up from the day-to-day experience of being a quad became internal scars—not visible to the naked eye. For a while after the accident, the feelings I expressed to everyone weren't entirely mine—concealing the sorrow, pain, and anxiety I felt so that everyone, especially my family, didn't experience them. Believing I could completely protect them from my despair was ridiculous because they often sensed it anyway. And pushing the emotional extremes deep down in the recesses of my mind wasn't okay. However, it worked for me, trying to control something. Anything. Still, harboring those emotions was difficult because they festered under the surface. This approach—dismissing the pain while actually feeling it—prevented me from sliding down the rabbit hole and losing my way.

Through the first years of my new life, acknowledging terms like *paralyzed* and *handicapped* was like owning a jacket lined with broken glass—impossible to wear. They were just words, but they defined weakness, brokenness, and how everyone viewed me now—my worsening perception giving me more reason to avoid my reality. To relinquish lingering despair and move forward, I had to truly mourn the loss of my old life. What defines each of us is different.

But most of what made me Non was stripped away by the accident. Eight or nine years passed before I could accept and integrate the definitions associated with disability without the cringe of denial.

Understanding the stages of loss helped. And the choice to live—not give up—helped too. As I loosened the grip on the heartache that makes you question your existence, I let go of an ideal expectation of how my life should work out.

Life is challenging. It isn't fair! But I hope that, by smiling to express happiness as I lean on faith, family, friendship, and everything that reminds me to be grateful for a difficult life, I remind patients, friends, family, and anyone who can feel my smile to be thankful. I will always ask questions. Am I such a terrible person that I deserve this? Why me and not the evil that goes unpunished or the million-dollar embezzler who never gets caught? These questions don't have answers that make sense. However, you slowly lose yourself when you embrace doubt rather than hope. You have to forgive yourself for whatever keeps you from moving forward. I had to shed my guilt.

When I forgave myself, my future didn't belong to tragedy anymore. The hard life I didn't plan for could be worthwhile and wonderful.

The impact of my disability on my family and everyone around me was not as horrible as I had imagined. Life has not been easy. But the influence of my life has been more good than bad, affecting more people who are struggling than I could have imagined.

My body is fragile, broken, in a wheelchair, unable to move. I cannot scratch my nose, feed myself, or do any of those things that we stop letting our moms see when we are 6 years old. I need help to go anywhere, and I often encounter obstacles preventing me from participating like everyone else. All of this, and more, describes who I am. But, most importantly, it does not define me.

Accepting my disability is part of my life story. I am grateful for all the unexpected blessings in my life. I still hide my pain to limit the influence. But joy and happiness are genuine now. I smile, laugh, and wink because I am thankful for where I am despite my injury. The first time I said that I was happy with where I was, it surprised me. I'm not pleased or glad the accident happened. But I am thankful for the amazing things that have happened since. I am grateful for all that I've learned over the years. I'm thankful for the friendships I've made.

The relationship that grew between Sylvia and me was something I couldn't have imagined. Even though she bore resentment and questioned everything early on, she took care of me with a dedication to keep me healthy and alive. As the newness of my broken body distorted the months after the accident, she persisted and didn't give up on me. Through the adversity and darkness of the nightmare, Sylvia and I started rebuilding a relationship we'd once lost. We made it through each day and grew closer and closer even though we struggled to understand any of it. And as the struggles scoured our hearts of what we were, we found strength in each other and nurtured something new.

Communication between us now feels ordinary. We don't tread into rough waters so deep that we drown. And like most people, we make up after a disagreement. It doesn't feel just normal, though. It feels like a love story to me. It is what I think others go through, with highs and lows, but with unconditional love that the fortunate find. That's why I wouldn't take it back—the terrible part of adversity, given where we are all these years later. All we've been through, the difficult parts included, brought Sylvia and me to a happy place in life. And she is the best of it all.

I feel immense satisfaction telling parts of our story to others in hospitals, at events, and schools. By sharing some of the feel-good moments that happened to us along the way, I'm reassured that my life has value and that our story can help others. I can laugh at being attacked by a kitten. I can laugh about having food prepared not the way I want or even being accidentally beaned in the face by stray wiffle balls. The accumulation of all the atypical experiences we have faced has created a normal for us and a story to share with others at schools, churches, Costco, and hospitals. These stories have hopefully inspired their lives.

I hope that patients, friends, and family have seen in me what is possible through something so difficult.

Elks Rehabilitation Hospital visits have been part of my routine for much of the last 20 years. Wheeling through the halls, spending time with patients and professionals, and wanting to make a difference have been an unexpected source of joy that has profoundly affected me. My need to belong—to impact others—like a job or being part of any team does, has positively provided structure, friendships, parenting skills, income, and so many good things. It has made me aware that something as simple as a kind gesture, like a smile, can inspire hope. When I visited Elks, healing and affecting change was the goal—to feel worthy because I didn't. My family wanted for me to be okay. So I stumbled forward, fell, and got back up. And I fulfilled many dreams I had for my younger self. I remembered that interacting is a part of who I am—who I was before the accident. That life is worth living no matter what is thrown at you. Reshaping my lost identity was another by-product of Elks' influence on me during all the years I volunteered. At first, identifying with my chair hurt. Then, I gained confidence in my wheelchair's role in my life—in part, because of the Elks.

The hospital was a starting point to engage random people with a wink and a smile, opening doors to some of the best conversations and encounters.

Costco

For a time, I also visited Costco almost every Saturday, creating more chances to engage with others. It isn't necessary to go to Costco as often as I did because no one needs that much toilet paper or laundry detergent. What IS pretty awesome about Costco, and why it is worth visiting weekly, is that you can have lots of food samples and a hot dog and drink for $1.50. You can also peruse the aisles like you might at a fair—even if you don't need four gallons of mayo or 850 gumballs. When I get there, the pick-me-up begins at the entrance, where my caregiver displays my Costco card, and the happy greeter acknowledges my shopping potential with a nod and smile.

The commotion at Costco is always provocative. The snack specials or the new tech in TVs at the entrance always entice you to stroll over and purchase that giant bag of jerky or at least to watch two minutes of *Shrek* on a giant screen. Patrons usually seem pleased to be there, wearing subtle grins. I also enjoy wheeling about the store to grab free samples or get a good deal for lunch. But I especially appreciate the interactions with shoppers and staff. You almost always run into someone you know, someone who knows you, or someone you get to know.

The start of most chance interactions often feels artificial, tainted by others' preconceptions of how I should feel about my wheelchair. Sometimes, I get the subtle head nod or the "I see you" gesture when I make eye contact with someone. Other times, it's the quick, polite smile that says, "I'm in a hurry." Both are fleeting. But now and then, I catch a glance long enough to be my playful self, pairing my smile with a wink. The reactions I get are surprising. The usual response isn't what you'd expect. I've had so many heartwarming conversations sparked by this simple gesture—conversations that have been both gratifying and validating. Comments like, "Thank you for your smile," "You look like you're up to something," or even, "Can I help you?"—often from people who are just passing by—always leave me feeling energized.

The interactions I value most are those that allow me to share a bit of myself with curious individuals who ask about my disability. People often notice wheelchair users first for being in the chair, and then for how well we maneuver it. Many are impressed with my backing-up skills. I'm always elated when someone approaches me out of curiosity, creating an opportunity to connect and converse.

An older gentleman once asked me, "Why are you smiling?" I responded with a smile and said, "Why not?" That simple exchange opened the door for him to ask about my injury. And soon I found myself sharing a brief history of my accident and life after. The assumption—or better, the stereotype—that a disabled person views life with a certain gloom is often false. Yes, we wrestle with a lot of exasperating challenges that most people don't face. But my response was a departure from that belief, and it seemed to leave an impression on my new Costco friend. His question was meant to convey a sense of connection, similar to how a handshake can put us at ease. He listened intently to my story, thanked me, and before leaving to find his wife, he placed his hand on mine and said, "Keep smiling." As he walked away, he took a tiny piece of me with him.

Over the years, I've made friends at Costco with both patrons and employees. I can't count how many interactions have made me look forward to Saturday road trips to the toilet paper-selling giant. And I have been recognized in the community by my chair, art, and even via those trips to the store. But some exchanges are more than life-affirming, connecting all the dots into one life-changing memory.

During a visit, while I was searching for something down a conveniently wide aisle, a woman I didn't recognize approached me. Thoughtful shoppers often ask if I need help when I'm alone, especially if they see me eyeing an item that I'm considering adding to our cart. Sometimes, I take them up on the offer and ask them to place it on my lap. Then I find Sylvia, who has no choice but to add it to the cart for all my diligent work—clever, right? But that wasn't the case with the stranger who walked up to me this time.

She approached with a smile. "Are you Non?" she asked. "Yes, ma'am," I replied. She continued, "You talked to my son about a year ago at Elks Rehabilitation Hospital, and I just wanted to thank you. Your visits to the hospital and talking to patients help—it makes a difference." What struck me most about her demeanor was the weight she seemed to carry, a kind of unspoken emotion conveyed through how close she stood, her facial expression, and the tone of her voice. After her kind words, I thanked her, still uncertain of who she was. Then she mentioned her son, Tony, and described why he had been in therapy at the hospital. I remembered and nodded. "Yeah, how's he doing?" I asked. She told me he had to have an amputation after all, but that he was doing okay.

The first time I spoke to her son, I was visiting another patient. By chance, I wheeled through the therapy gym, where Tony was interacting with a physical therapist friend. Joe, the therapist, grabbed my attention and introduced us, just as he had done with other patients before. After the introduction and a brief pause—so I didn't come across as too intrusive—I asked Tony why he was there. He nonchalantly described an unfortunate accident at work that had required multiple painful surgeries. Though he made light of most of it and joked a lot, it was clear he was wrestling with something deeper.

It usually takes a while to develop a rapport, but I have to admit, I liked Tony right away. We quickly connected because we shared similar challenging experiences. Tony was honest as he spoke about his injury, and I wanted to stay longer to continue our conversation. However, I had other errands to take care of. So, as I prepared to leave, I asked if he would be returning for more treatment so we could talk again. Joe informed me that Tony would be receiving therapy twice a week for at least a couple of months. I decided to return twice the following week to visit him. And after that, I saw him a few more times whenever I could.

During our visits at Elks, Tony brought levity with his attitude and laughter. He talked about his mom and her worries for him, his friends, and his passion for fixing cars. In return, I shared stories about my family, my accident and disability, and my art. It was easy to be around him. When I didn't see him after his last outpatient therapy session, I remained hopeful that he would be okay, even though I never really know what happens after patients move on.

So, when his mom approached me at Costco several months later, she offered me a gift as she began to fill in the weeks after Tony and I first met. I felt a bit relieved when she mentioned that what I did for him at Elks Rehab Hospital had helped. She told me that when Tony first went to the hospital for therapy, he was ready to give up. He was in so much pain from all the surgeries they had performed to save his leg that he was struggling. She said, "Before he met you at Elks, Tony told me he was sorry but he couldn't take it anymore. He didn't want to deal with the pain any longer."

She was emotional as she explained that he had even secured a means to end his life. In truth, he'd said goodbye before heading to his appointment the day we met. Because of the pain she saw him in, how discouraged he was, and his feeling that there was no end in sight, she was worried something tragic was inevitable.

"After he met and talked to you at the hospital that day, he didn't say much to me when he arrived home, just that he met this guy in a wheelchair. But he didn't act quite like before. Something changed. Then, after a couple of weeks of visiting with you, he told me I didn't have to worry anymore. I'm not sure what would have happened. But I believe you helped prevent something terrible from happening."

The emotional facade transformed after her story, as she continued to fill in the months after her son and I met. We both took in big cleansing breaths as she finished. And the exhale contained the sadness she used to feel for her son. His perseverance and acceptance of losing his leg were parts of my story too. The connection, the brief time I spent with him receiving more than giving, was uplifting when she shared comical stories about his recovery instead of gloomy ones. I tried to keep from becoming overtly emotional, understanding that when she approached me, gratitude and hope represented the interaction.

Constantly aware of my disability's impact on everything, as those thoughts live in the recesses of my mind, I reach for them when I'm down and more pensive than I should be. But I think of the people I've shared with and connected with along the way.

The effects of my wheelchair on everyone I encounter seem to dictate the conversations and interactions we have. Even at a distance, my appearance is first defined by wheels, metal, plastic, and a disability—things I have no control of. But when I converse with anyone, a smile can certainly make a difference.

Chapter 13

The Blessings

In 2004, my friend George introduced me to the Free Wheelchair Mission during an occupational therapy conference. There were many attendees from all over the Northwest, including many from Elks, most of whom significantly helped shape my sense of purpose over the years. I cherished the opportunity to show my art and be among friends at the event.

When George arrived during setup the first day, the usual friendly banter ensued between us—more me giving him a hard time. However, he wasn't up for the usual jabs. Instead, he was proudly showing off a wheelchair he purchased online, not related to the seminar. And his enthusiasm was evident.

He had mentioned his new find a week earlier—only to be met with skepticism from me. "They took your money, George. You were scammed," I quipped. And his playful response, "Are you ever going to grow up?" made me laugh enough to stop.

So, he was happy to show me the wheelchair that day. He had this "See! It's not a scam" grin as he unveiled it like a brand new car on *The Price Is Right*. In the same breath, he also confessed that it took him longer to piece together than it should have—a detail I used to tease him about further. Despite that, he was eager to tell me ALL about it.

The wheelchair George displayed consisted of two bicycle tires, two industrial casters, a white plastic resin chair with the legs sawn off, and shaped tubing. It was uncomplicated yet ingenious. As we sat there before everything started, George told a story of how Don Shoendorfer, an engineer traveling in Morocco, observed a disabled woman crawling on the ground, enduring verbal and physical abuse, blamed for her station in life. Don was saddened by how she lived and the burden she and others coped with. And he felt inspired to help and find a way to change the lives of people like her.

Following his travels, Don spent months crafting a functional, affordable wheelchair, hoping to lift people off the ground. He had found a calling—a way to use his many gifts to make a difference. The work came together quickly. And not long after, he delivered his first few chairs to India in 2001. In so doing, the Free Wheelchair

Mission was born to provide wheelchairs for those who crawl on the ground.

George continued talking about the chair and the possibilities. Moved by the story, he soon expressed his desire to be part of this open-handed cause. And yes, I thought it was too good to be true.

George's reaction was no surprise since it's how he lives—eager to give back and help others. His enthusiasm drew me in. Much of my life unfolded quite differently from what I had imagined, certain that I was constrained by my disability. So, the prospect of helping people in distant lands was inviting. Again, something stirred in me. So I agreed to participate in any way I could.

Following the seminar, George shared the Free Wheelchair Mission's cause and the unique wheelchair with Pastor Donald Batubenga, his wife, Julienne, and New Hearts Ministries International—a refugee church he was a part of. Inspired, they echoed a desire to be a part of what was becoming a team. Moreover, Pastor Donald and the New Hearts church provided the first few wheelchairs from the Treasure Valley. The group had come together surprisingly fast—undeniably because the cause was very personal to the refugee church. Because of George's conviction, Idaho Believes was born.

George needed a goal for us to strive toward—to get Idaho Believes started and motivated. And he came up with an idea that married his love of Boise State Football to the Free Wheelchair Mission's cause. Since we're ALL Bronco fans, he suggested we try to provide one wheelchair to lift someone off the ground for as many seats as there are in BSU's football stadium. At the time, there were 36,387 seats in the facility. With that number in mind, the group began visiting churches, groups, and anyone who would listen, raising donations.

During each presentation, George passionately expressed his commitment to helping lift people off the ground. He conveyed to the audiences that the cost to build and transport a wheelchair was less than the price of a family dinner. And every congregation, audience, and attendee who listened to George speak about the Free Wheelchair Mission was amazed that such a modest sum could change someone's life so profoundly.

With their hearts touched, chairs were gifted, one at a time, as we shared Don's mission. Others joined the cause as well. The hospital where George worked decided to support our endeavor by printing one thousand copies of a picture I painted for the Free Wheelchair Mission. This organization was inspired by the mission and used my painting as a way to represent their passion. When someone donated enough for a chair, they were given a painting as a token of appreciation for their generosity.

Twenty years before, I entertained the belief that I could affect change while giving my high school graduation speech—or at the very least, I hoped I could. I certainly didn't believe that impacting people around the world was possible. But that small bit of hope suddenly meant something tangible two decades later. Never in my life could I have imagined being a part of something like this.

The Free Wheelchair Mission's outreach spans the globe, delivering mobility to those confined to life on the ground. Not long after the inception of Idaho Believes—after sharing the group's hope to people in the Treasure Valley and beyond—George and other members of our group began traveling to distant lands with the Free Wheelchair Mission to help distribute the first shipments from Idaho.

The life-changing power of each wheelchair reshapes my perspective on the blessings and privileges I often take for granted.

The recipients' gratitude and emotions reveal what a wheelchair means to someone who has been living on the ground—their lives transformed as they are elevated away from rejection, shame, and humiliation. Each chair becomes a beacon of hope, a testament to the ripple effect of even the smallest deeds—a wheelchair, smile, or wink. They serve as a poignant reminder of all I have and the potential for positive change by any one person.

Such is the narrative passed down by parents, teachers, and role models: that we can change the world. However, when life is marked by personal struggles and witnessing the suffering of others, selflessness can feel like a daunting task. For a long time, I doubted my ability to impact others, feeling more than just physically paralyzed.

But in moments when I've shared with congregations, I've found myself uplifted. I am deeply moved by the generosity of those who donate to provide a wheelchair for someone they will never meet—their kindness is inspiring.

Though my role within this group may feel small, the knowledge that lives around the world are transformed through these gifts affirms that even the smallest effort matters. With every chair given, I feel a bit more capable—less disabled. The impact the Free Wheelchair Mission has on others, and on me, has truly been life-affirming.

ART

When I first rediscovered art, I couldn't yet see the profound role it would play in my life. From those first hesitant scribbles when George set his custom easel in front of me to the finished pieces I later created, art became both therapy and inspiration as I confronted my new reality. It gave me something tangible, a way to fill time with purpose. Drawing with my mouth reminded me that I was still capable. Slowly, as I created, my confidence began to return. Each stroke—no matter how small—helped transform me.

Just like when Jacob asked me to scratch his back, my art was a turning point. Art, in ways I hadn't anticipated, began to foster healing between Jacob and me. When I scratched his back, I began figuring out how to be his father again. Jacob had witnessed my earliest attempts at drawing with a mouth stick, and he wanted to help me with it. Through that shared experience, art connected us, becoming a source of accomplishment for both father and son.

Art did more than rebuild my self-esteem. It became a way to connect with others. I used it as a conversation starter with patients, inadvertently showing them, "See what is possible?" Given my insecurity, it felt a bit gimmicky, sure, but it worked. Patients and therapists responded—not just to what I painted but to how I painted. Eventually, I even earned some income from my art. But more importantly, it became part of something larger, something more meaningful.

Art didn't immediately define my life. However, it became an essential outlet—much like working out to stay healthy or reading to keep the mind sharp. Over time, it wove itself into every aspect of my life, bringing my family closer and offering me new ways to engage with the world.

My connection to the Free Wheelchair Mission is deeply tied to this artistic journey. Through art, I began to understand my place in the world, my relationship with time, and what it meant to be present. With art, I realized I had more available time than many others—not just for painting but for being there for people in ways that mattered.

The small successes with art—a new technique suggested by a friend or a meaningful conversation sparked by my work—became personal victories. Art provided a mental escape, a way to connect with people, and a sense of purpose. Each painting introduced me to someone new, someone inspired by my journey. Their admiration fed my confidence and deepened my connection to society. In many ways, painting became a catalyst for change in my life, helping me adapt and grow as a disabled person.

When I first heard the word ***quadriplegic*** used in reference to myself, it hit me with a mix of fear and grim understanding—I knew my life would be forever changed. My health would be precarious, always teetering on a razor's edge. Blood pressure issues, the constant threat of pneumonia, and an internal struggle with my emotions made long-term plans feel out of reach.

But the physical challenges were only part of the isolation. The loss of familiar routines—work, golfing with friends, or visiting favorite spots—left me disconnected from the world. I longed for a different past, present, and future. Through this new reality, art became a lifeline, helping me set aside the despair that could have consumed me. Through art, I found a way to participate in life again. It became a bridge to the outside world, giving me a reason to feel alive.

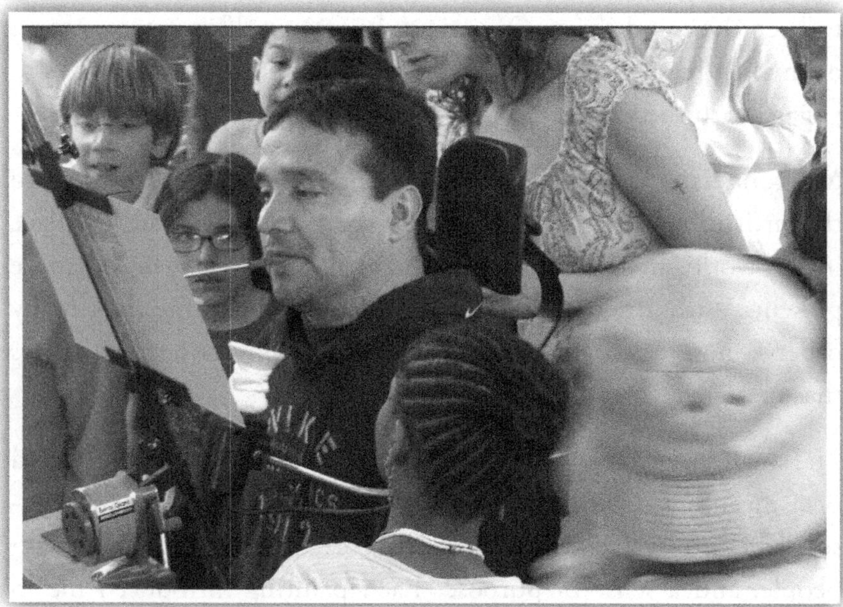

Art, in part, filled the voids that physical limitations left behind. It became a cornerstone of my psychological, emotional, and even physical well-being—a vital connection between the many facets of my existence.

Family and Gratitude

Throughout these years, my wife, kids, friends, and caregivers—sometimes even strangers—remind me, in small ways, how blessed my life has been. A kiss, a smile, a thoughtful call, or a visit pulls me back to the present, away from distant longings, and fills my heart with gratitude.

My family has expanded once again to now include grandchildren. My grandson, sitting beside me as I help with his homework, shows me how fortunate I am. Watching him have water balloon fights with Sylvia, or making silly duck noises to get a smile from my granddaughter, fills me with joy. Conversations with my daughter about school, world events, and her track meets fuel me to keep fighting the good fight. And when my son asks for a quick golf lesson before a tournament, it brings me happiness words can't fully capture.

One truth has persisted over these past three decades: the constant weighing of ability versus inability. It's a brain game I play, and though exhausting, it has proven to be both a challenge and a gift. Dreaming that I might hold my grandchildren or wrap my arms around my wife sustains me, even though the dreams hurt. Yet, through it all, the optimist in me has managed to keep the shadows at bay long enough to add each good moment—every lesson and positive feeling—to the light side of the scale. And they've begun to add up.

Inadequacy still lingers at times, but I've learned it's okay to feel flawed. I don't beat myself up when I feel vulnerable, because everyone faces insecurities at some point.

I've also learned to laugh at the awkwardness of my life. There's humor in the messiness. An unexpected burp or a booger I can't wipe from my nose might seem undignified. But these moments remind me that I'm human. (Though blaming a deaf board member with a sideways, it-was-him head nod after I let out a "small toot" might not have been my finest moment.)

What isn't okay, though, is letting others carry the weight of my struggle. A friend once told me that I was "blessed with a burden." At first, I wasn't sure what he meant. But now I understand that this burden—my disability—touches those around me too. Acknowledging that truth means making a choice—let the burden define me or choose gratitude.

Choosing Gratitude

The past 30 years have been full of highs and lows. But I am grateful for every day I get out of bed. Each morning serves as a reminder of how fortunate I am.

Choosing gratitude not only lightens my load, but it also eases the burden on my family, especially Sylvia. I hope it also inspires others to embrace thankfulness —because gratitude is a blessing.

Every sunrise is an opportunity to make a difference. Today matters because none of us know when it might be our last. And that's why my choice—every day—is gratitude.

Conclusion

For Sylvia

Consumed by an internal debate following the accident, I lay in bed each day, driven to the edge as I struggled with a lifetime of loss and abandonment. The first weeks at St. Luke's Hospital, and then at Rancho, were impossible. But nurses, staff members, and other patients kept me from the abyss. Then, a respiratory therapist helped me feel a mustard seed of hope.

At home, an occupational therapist, caregivers, friends, and family encouraged me to stay. Still, trapped in a small, crowded bedroom, I felt different—unworthy, even though I wasn't.

The fear that I had lost the ability to be a good father, husband, or someone capable of living a worthy life compounded my understanding of my life's meaning. Worse, the insecurities caused by the accident, combined with broken childhood memories, led to a strange dependence on sorrow. I was unwilling to relinquish sadness for fear that things could get worse.

The inevitable acceptance of the words FOREVER PARALYZED felt as isolating and demeaning as a solitary walk with no one to speak to, ever. But that acceptance was also necessary to move on.

To keep from fading away to nothing, I had to manage my despair. Sullen faces of family and friends ushered me through the first few months of my altered reality, as the guilt I felt for every past failure and present situation festered, preventing healing. The loss of my identity defined every minute that ticked by as I could only imagine a broken body and a fractured future.

Then Jacob helped focus my vision. And Sylvia dug her heels in while our family and friends continued bolstering our efforts to cope.

Slowly, love, faith, and laughter nourished hope for the future. The best things in life, what we all need to be happy, were always there, even though we may have been too blind, young, or preoccupied to see them.

The simplest pleasures, feeling the sun on your face or receiving a loving smile, are taken for granted and unappreciated. But they are all around us! These reasons— these moments—are enough to live for if we acknowledge them. The accident became an unexpected blessing as it challenged me to remember this.

Suddenly, we had endured one moment at a time for over 30 years.

I have experienced a wide range of emotions in my life: fear, abandonment, and so much pain that sometimes it's hard to breathe. Despite being broken and leading a completely different life from my old one, throughout all of it, someone was always there for me. The one feeling of desperation I never truly experienced was feeling completely alone. I didn't need saving, but I craved that hug from her. I haven't felt completely alone because, from my perspective, I have not been. Sylvia was always there.

The Cool Side of the Pillow

There are irksome consolations one has to make with quadriplegia—accepting your limitations is front and center. However, I am fortunate to have all my needs met. I still experience many of life's pleasures like everyone else, such as:

When my nose unplugs itself.
Hearing the right song at the right moment.
Freshly baked cookies.
The smell of freshly cut grass.
That first sip of coffee in the morning.
Waking up next to someone I love.
My wife's tender embrace.

However, there are some of life's simplest pleasures that I cannot experience, such as:

Finding $10 in my pocket.
A shower and beer after a workout or run.
Scratching that itch that is *really* hard to access
. . . scratching any itch, for that matter.
Taking a bath and then going straight to sleep in a freshly made bed.
Flipping to the cool side of the pillow.

Spending the majority of my day in bed makes the cool side of the pillow experience especially woeful. But having a pillow placed on the side of my face is a consolation. I can feel the cool side for a bit right after I lay down.

Last night, Sylvia awoke to go to the bathroom and check on our dog. As she crawled back in bed, I asked, "Are you okay?" She said, "Yeah." And then she reached over and flipped my pillow.

Afterword

By George Hage

When Idaho Believes came together in 2004, Non had a significant part, not only with his art, but in sharing his story and his desire to be involved with this vital cause. Non, always so articulate, told heart-warming stories and was eager to share. When it became more difficult for Non to attend our local presentations, I made sure his prints were available to donors and that Non was included in the PowerPoint presentations I would share.

I began traveling with Free Wheelchair Mission in 2006, where I was introduced to what I call "this other world." On my initial trip to Uganda, following the distribution of 550 wheelchairs around the country, I got my first taste of how common it was to see people crawling (80 million people in the world according to WHO). We went to seven different locations in the Ugandan bush where large groups of hopeful recipients would be lifted off the ground into their brand-new wheelchairs. But before anyone received a wheelchair, customary speeches were given. Caught off guard on my first wheelchair distribution, I was introduced to the crowd as an ambassador from America with a message to share. But I didn't come with a message and didn't plan on sharing. What would I say to the 110 people on the ground in front of me that crawled or were carried all their lives in third world poverty, frequently told they were "cursed by God" and a "burden on society"?

Who was I to give a pep talk, a nugget of professional advice, or even an ounce of encouragement? Thankfully, as I walked toward the mic, I thought of Non's story; how an accident left him completely paralyzed below his neck, unable to raise an arm, bend a finger, or move a toe. I shared how he was completely dependent, unable to feed himself, wash his face, or hold his child. But, when he was told about people in Africa, and other parts of the world, who needed wheelchairs, he did what he was able to do—he painted with his mouth and continued to be an encourager to all those whom God put in his life. With the inspiration of Non's story and the answered prayer of sitting in their own new wheelchairs, the future began to appear hopeful for all the recipients. I'd never seen joy so animated and pure as I did on that day and will never forget the feeling of not wanting to leave the celebration.

We had six more wheelchair distributions over the next few days, and six more when we returned to Uganda the next year. Every time I shared Non's story, the translators had no idea what I meant by "paint with his mouth." They often stopped translating and stared at me with a blank look on their face. Putting a pen in my mouth, I would demonstrate by making strokes in the air. They were greatly inspired and encouraged to know they had an advocate and friend in America that understood their suffering and was fighting for them. In those two visits to Uganda, I shared Non's story to almost 1,000 people who crawled through third world poverty. They often cheered for Non and celebrated by singing, clapping, and dancing in their wheelchairs. Non's message of encouragement, dignity, and hope seemed to resonate with those with disabilities in "this other world."

The more I traveled with Free Wheelchair Mission, the more I told Non's story and shared his artwork. I also heard more and more stories from those receiving wheelchairs. So many young women in Uganda were handed their babies as soon as they were lifted into their wheelchairs. It was then I understood these women crawled all through their pregnancies. One woman told us she crawled through six pregnancies, another crawled through her pregnancy with twins. In Somalia, I asked a 13-year-old girl with cerebral palsy why she wanted a wheelchair. Her answer was simply, "I just want to go outside." Too difficult for her mother to carry, and unable to crawl, 13-year-old Kaudra had already become a shut in, something very common in "this other world."

In Uganda and India, we gave wheelchairs to recipients who crawled for over 50 years and one wheelchair was given to man who crawled for 80. For millions of people, their whole world extends only as far as they can crawl, but the wheelchair greatly expands their territory and opens a new world of opportunities. One young man took off as soon as he received his wheelchair, pushing as fast as he could go. We caught up a mile down the road and yelled out to him as he raced by, "Where ya going?" His excited response, "I don't know, I've never been this far before."

I gave one of Non's prints to a pastor in Uganda that crawled all his life, including every Sunday, in front of his congregation, before preaching his sermon. As he was lifted into his wheelchair for the first time he proclaimed, "This wheelchair will be my pulpit." While in Nicaragua, on another trip, I met Pastor Miguel while visiting patients in a rehab hospital. He and six other patients were crammed in a very crowded room. Twenty-two years earlier, he was on top of his roof, trying to repair a leak when he fell to the ground, breaking his back. He became a paraplegic, paralyzed from the mid-trunk down. He was given a used wheelchair in poor condition that lasted less than two years, spending the next 20 years in bed or on a chair next to the bed. After telling him the story of the pastor from Uganda, Pastor Miguel transferred into his new wheelchair and, with a smile, repeated the words, "This will be my pulpit." I recently gave all three of Non's prints to a young, indigenous teenage girl, receiving her wheelchair high up in the Andes Mountains of Peru. Since we knew her name ahead of time, Non was able to sign a personal note to her in Spanish.

In Kigali, Rwanda, speaking to a class of 35 World Vision employees at a training session, we had a handsome, middle-aged man in a wheelchair come to visit. He had been an officer in the Rwandan army during the genocide of 1994. At the start of the war, he broke his back in a jeep accident, becoming a paraplegic. He then lived the next 15 years in a hospital in Kigali and the following five years in an apartment connected to the hospital. His doctors didn't believe he could survive a complete spinal cord injury, in Rwanda, apart from a hospital setting. He was in an agitated mood that morning when he wheeled into the classroom. But after seeing a video of

Non painting and sharing words of hope, his whole persona was transformed. When he was given one of Non's prints to take home, he became deeply emotional and grabbing the mic, he expressed his heartfelt gratitude and thankfulness for what he experienced that day. I could only imagine how difficult his life had been the last 20 years, but at that moment, the weight had been lifted.

In east Africa, we conducted a training with our partners Agape Mobility Ethiopia. Because of ongoing war throughout the region, we weren't allowed to distribute wheelchairs outside the capital of Ethiopia, Addis Ababa. We held both our training and wheelchair distribution at the Red Cross Center where medics were training to receive casualties of the war. I wondered how many new casualties would be receiving these wheelchairs. On the morning of the last day of the training, I showed a five-minute video of Non painting and sharing his story of hope. That was followed by 15 minutes of heartfelt questions concerning Non's life, handled by our wonderful interpreter and physical therapist, Sofonias. There was a quick review of everything they learned that week about assembly and fitting recipients in wheelchairs, followed by a written test. Then came the arrival of the recipients, crawling, hobbling and being carried into the courtyard where they would be custom fit with their own wheelchair. There was joy in the courtyard that day as recipients and their families left with dignity, mobility, and hope for the future. And there was joy in the classroom when those who completed the training knew they had personally transformed someone's life and will have the opportunity to impact lives again and again and again as more containers of wheelchairs arrive. As each student's name was called, they came forward to receive a certificate for completing the training and were surprised to also receive one of Non's prints. The photo I took that day is one of my favorites. Non's artistry was the perfect touch on this special day.

We recently celebrated the 20th anniversary of Idaho Believes. Non has joined us whenever he was able, presenting at churches, schools, hospitals, businesses, service organizations, and with other nonprofits. One church, Eagle Hills Church, has supported us for 18 years, donating over 2,700 wheelchairs. And one of our most memorable fundraisers was held by Game Changers Idaho, a local nonprofit that provides the opportunity for kids with and without special needs to participate together in sporting events. The founder, Gabe Moreno, came to visit me one day, stating he would like to empower his kids by raising funds to provide wheelchairs for children in other countries. They put on a track event and raised enough for 34 children to have wheelchairs. Each of the athletes received medals and then heard Non's story as they chose one of Non's prints to take home. The next year, Gabe took a team to Lima, Peru to put on a sports camp for kids with disabilities.

Non's first two prints donated to Free Wheelchair Mission were of cascading waterfalls, rugged boulders, trees clinging to cliffs, and a beautiful array of color throughout. Non's third, and most popular, is Jesus pushing someone in a wheelchair down the path of life and on to eternity. He placed the words of Jesus at the bottom of the print: "I'll be with you." That print is not only found in many nations of the developing world through Non's connection with Free Wheelchair Mission, but also the countries of 25 Mandela/ Washington Fellows from all over Africa. They heard his story and took this print back to their nations following the completion of their internship and commencement ceremony at Boise State University in 2020.

As Non continues to thrive in a world where he's been denied so many basic abilities and activities of life that most all of us take for granted, he continues to be an amazing husband, father, grandfather, and friend. He loves to coach, loves to tease, loves to have conversations, loves to teach, loves to create, loves to watch movies and sports, loves to hang out with friends and family. He loves to make people smile, laugh, and overcome adversities. I believe Non loves people and loves life. Even though life has been so difficult, he continues to live fully to the glory of God. He continues to spread faith, comfort and hope in the Treasure Valley, as well as in faraway places, reminding others by the way he chooses to live that you don't have to wheel down that path alone.

"Be strong and courageous! Do not be afraid or discouraged. For the Lord your God is with you wherever you go." (Joshua 1:9 NLT)

Non is loved by thousands of individuals and has made his mark worldwide. Now that is an unexpected ride.

For more information on Idaho Believes,
Free Wheelchair Mission or to make a donation,
scan the QR code below.

Acknowledgments

This book is the culmination of countless moments of love, encouragement, and unwavering support, and I want to take this opportunity to express my deepest gratitude.

First and foremost, I thank my family: my wife, Sylvia, whose steadfast love and resilience have been my anchor; our son, Jacob, whose laughter and light inspire me to see the world as a place of possibility; my daughter, Isabella, whose strength, love, and grit bring joy to my life; and my wonderful grandson and granddaughter, who remind me daily of the beauty and promise of the future. To my extended family, thank you for lifting me up through every challenge and celebrating each victory as your own.

To George Hage, your friendship has been one of the greatest gifts of my life. Your foreword not only honors our shared journey but also perfectly captures the essence of this book. Thank you for believing in me and for sharing my story with others. Your wisdom, compassion, and enduring encouragement mean more than words can express.

I am immensely grateful to Maryanna Young, Beth Berger, Jennifer Regner, Mercy Sorich, Rachel Langaker, and the entire team at

Aloha Publishing. Your faith in this manuscript and your tireless efforts to bring it to life have been extraordinary. Your guidance, creativity, and collaboration have made this book a reality. Thank you for your passion and dedication, which shine through every page.

Finally, to all who have walked beside me, prayed for me, and shared their hearts and kindness in even the smallest moments, you are part of this journey. Your support has been a beacon in the darkness, reminding me that we are never truly alone.

This book is as much yours as it is mine. Together, we continue to ride this unexpected path, celebrating the beauty of life even in its most challenging moments.

With heartfelt gratitude,

About the Author

Hernan "Non" Reyes is an artist, advocate, and storyteller whose life embodies resilience, creativity, and service. In 1992, a motor vehicle accident left Non paralyzed from the shoulders down and unable to breathe on his own. Facing unimaginable challenges, he turned to his family and faith to rebuild his life and find purpose in the midst of adversity.

During his recovery, Non discovered a talent for art, using a brush or pencil held between his teeth to create stunning works of art. What began as therapeutic self-expression evolved into a powerful medium for inspiring others. His art not only captures beauty but also serves as a testament to the ability to transform life's obstacles into opportunities for growth.

Beyond his artistry, Non has dedicated much of his life to advocacy for individuals with disabilities. Early in his journey, he began visiting rehabilitation hospitals to encourage and uplift newly injured patients and their families. Speaking from personal experience, he offered practical insights, heartfelt stories, and hope for brighter days ahead. His outreach has made him a beloved figure in the Treasure Valley community and beyond.

Non's impact extended to a global stage through his work with the Free Wheelchair Mission. His story and art have become a beacon of hope for people with disabilities in developing countries. From Uganda to Nicaragua, Non's prints and messages of faith have inspired thousands.

Non is blessed with a loving family: his wife, Sylvia, their son, Jacob, their daughter, Isabella, and a grandson and granddaughter (pictured below). They have been his unwavering support system, and he credits them for his ability to find joy and purpose in life.

Today, Non continues to inspire through his art and advocacy. His love for others shines through in every brushstroke, every story he shares, and every life he touches. Whether creating paintings of breathtaking landscapes, encouraging others to overcome adversity, or simply bringing a smile to someone's face with a well-timed wink, Non's legacy is one of courage, faith, and compassion. He reminds us all that no matter the challenges we face, we don't have to walk—or wheel—through life alone.

Connect With the Author

Thank you for reading *An Unexpected Ride*. If Non's story inspired you, here are some simple ways to help spread the word and support his work:

Buy in bulk quantities of 25, 50, 100 or 500 to use as awareness materials or donor gifts at your organization

Share a picture of the book and tag @nonsmouthart

Leave a review on Amazon or Goodreads

Purchase Non's artwork at site.nonsmouthart.com

Recommend the book to a friend

Visit www.site.nonsmouthart.com to connect, explore Non's art, and learn more.

Share this message of hope and purpose to make a difference in the world!

aloha
PUBLISHING

Made in the USA
Monee, IL
06 May 2025